Table of contents

Welcome to Chiron Publications, serving the Jungian community for over 40 years!

We have over 300 books to browse. Please take special notice of our new releases and featured titles. Visit our website regularly, chironpublications.com, and sign-up to be on our email list to see the latest books, special offers, lectures and ordering options online.

LIBRARIES

Chiron Publications has been serving libraries with high quality hardcover non-fiction books concerning Mythology, Psychology, Personal growth, Inspiration, Spirituality, the Arts, as well as numerous other important subjects. We understand the importance of libraries and their role in training future generations of undergraduate and graduate students, and to support scholarship within the academics.

Chiron is pleased to offer trade discount pricing for verified libraries. Please call us at (828) 333-4787 or email us at generalmanager@chironpublications.com to register as a library and receive our full offerings of available titles.

BOOKSTORES

Chiron Publications has been serving bookstores for over 40 years with high quality Jungian books that foster deep insights and psychological awareness in their readers. All books are available at trade discount and may be ordered directly online. Please call us at (828) 333-4787 or email us at generalmanager@chironpublications.com to register and receive your unique discount code.

SUBMISSIONS

While many of Chiron Publications authors are Jungian analysts, we seek to be inclusive of authors with a Jungian, depth-psychological orientation who are making significant contributions to the field. Chiron Publications only accepts completed, well-edited manuscripts. For additional information, please visit chironpublications.com/submission-guidelines/.

Book information and prices are subject to change.

The Collected Works of Marie-Louise von Franz

The Collected Works of Marie-Louise von Franz is a 28 volume Magnum Opus from one of the leading minds in Jungian Psychology. The first volume, **Archetypal Symbols in Fairytales: The Profane and Magical Worlds**, released on von Franz's 106th birthday, January 4th, 2021 and is to be followed by 27 more volumes over the next 10-12 years. Volume 2 looks at the hero's journey, while Volume 3 explores the maiden's quest. Five of the 28 volumes have already been released with an anticipated schedule of 2-3 new volumes per year.

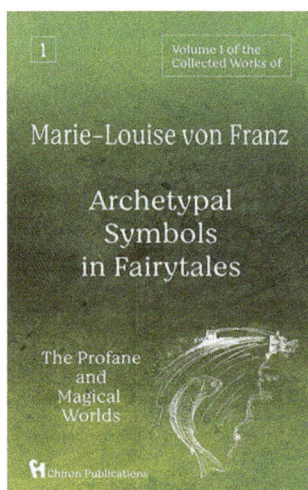

Volume 1
Archetypal Symbols in Fairytales:
The Profane and Magical Worlds

Fairytales, like myths, provide a cultural and societal backdrop that helps the human imagination narrate the meaning of life's events. The remarkable similarities in fairytale motifs across different lands and cultures inspired many scholars to search for the original homeland of fairytales.

Paperback
978-1-63051-854-7 $42.00
Hardcover
978-1-63051-855-4 $69.00

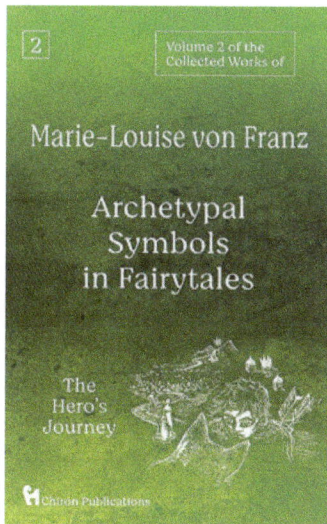

Volume 2
Archetypal Symbols in Fairytales: The Hero's Journey

The Hero's Journey is about the great adventure that leads to a cherished and difficult to obtain prize. In these fairytales, the Self is often symbolized as that treasured prize and the hero's travails symbolize the process of individuation. In its many manifestations, the hero embodies the emerging personality.

Paperback
978-1-63051-950-6 $42.00
Hardcover
978-1-63051-951-3 $69.00

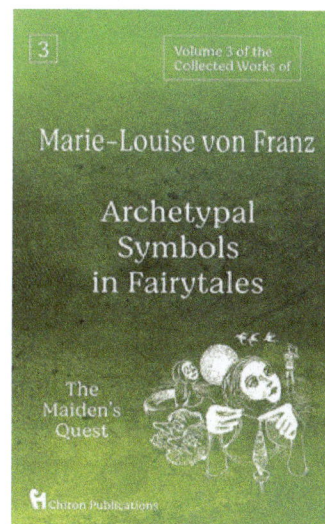

Volume 3
Archetypal Symbols in Fairytales: The Maiden's Quest

Volume 3 is a masterwork of cross-cultural scholarship, penetrating psychological insight, and a strikingly illuminating treatise. With her usual perspicacity and thoroughness, von Franz gathers countless fairytale motifs revealing a myriad of facets to the maiden's quest.

Paperback
978-1-63051-960-5 $42.00
Hardcover
978-1-63051-961-2 $69.00

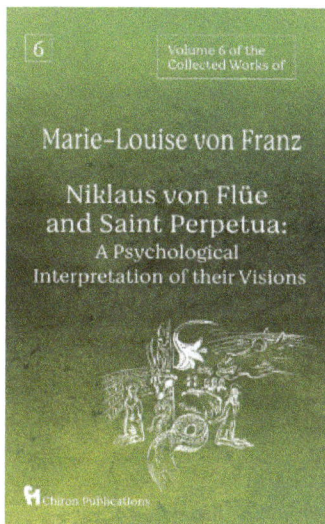

Volume 6
Niklaus Von Flüe And Saint Perpetua: A Psychological Interpretation of Their Visions

Volume 6 heralds translations of material never before available in English. It explores the profound visions of two ground-breaking saints in the Catholic church, Saint Niklaus von Flüe and Saint Perpetua.

Paperback
978-1-68503-029-2 $37.00
Hardcover
978-1-68503-030-8 $57.00

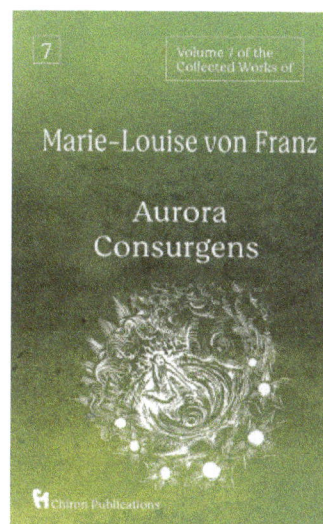

Volume 7
Aurora Consurgens

This medieval alchemical text is rich in symbolism and offers a glimpse into how unconscious contents can be understood through their interactions with the material world.

Paperback
978-1-63051-962-9 $52.00
Hardcover
978-1-63051-963-6 $77.00

The Collected Writings of Murray Stein

Chiron Publications is honored to publish the Collected Writings of Murray Stein.

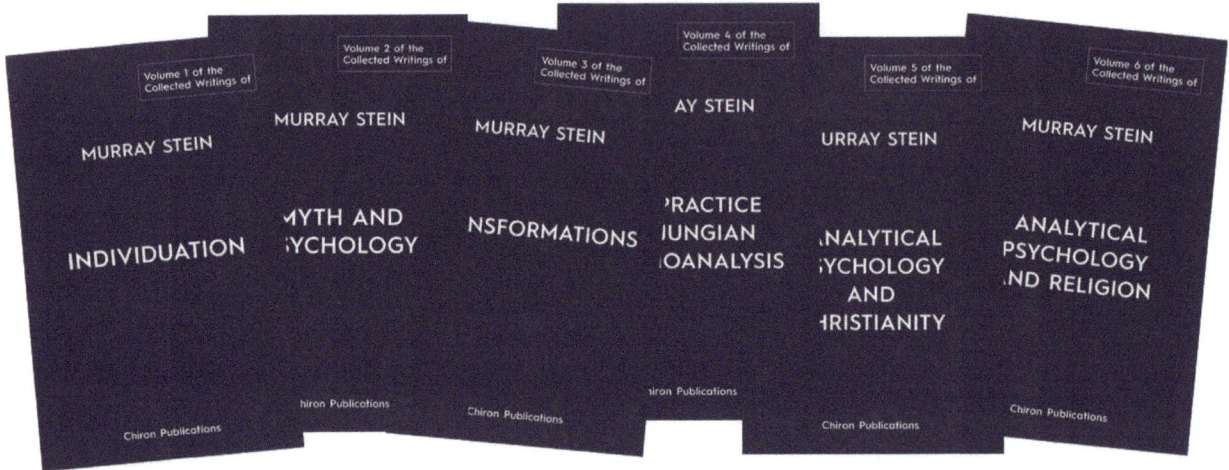

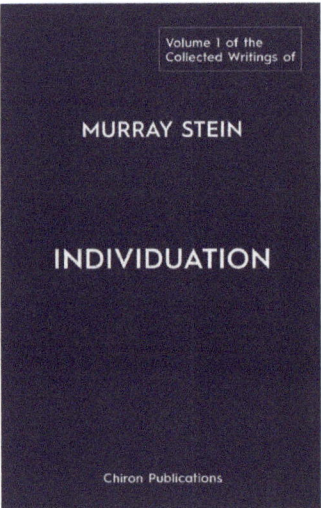

Volume 1
Individuation

Volume 1 contains a core element of Dr. Stein's lifelong teaching, namely the concept of individuation. The process of individuation fosters the fulfillment of unconscious potential as called forth by the archetypal Self.

Paperback
978-1-63051-760-1 $37.00
Hardcover
978-1-63051-761-8 $75.00

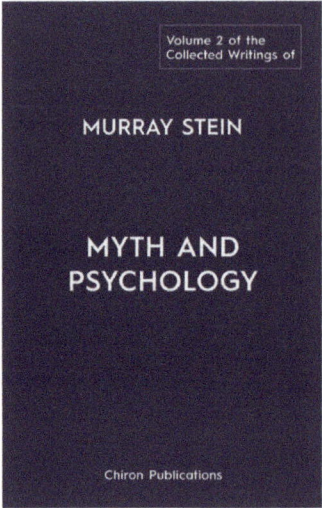

Volume 2
Myth and Psychology

Volume 2 looks at Mythology through a Jungian lens. Dr. Stein examines a vast array of mythologic figures. Mythology is ripe with transformative symbols reaching deep into our unconscious.

Paperback
978-1-63051-871-4 $37.00
Hardcover
978-1-63051-872-1 $75.00

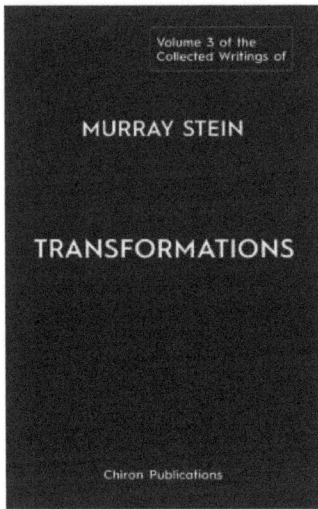

Volume 3
Transformations

Transformation suggests a profound change in life, often of a psychological or spiritual nature. In Volume 3, Dr. Stein examines this developmental process on a personal as well as a cultural level.

Paperback
978-1-63051-941-4 $39.00
Hardcover
978-1-63051-942-1 $75.00

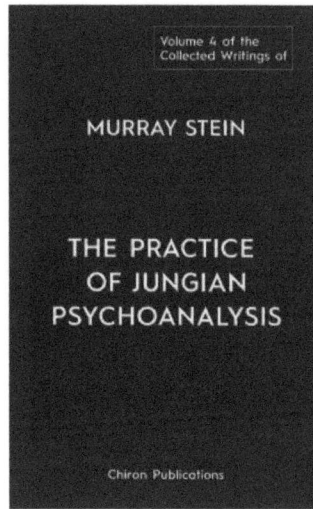

Volume 4
The Practice of Jungian Psychoanalysis

This is a practical volume, indispensable for Jungian analysts, Jungian psychotherapists or students hoping to sharpen their analytical skills. It is truly the "nuts and bolts" of Jungian analytical practice.

Paperback
978-1-68503-035-3 $37.00
Hardcover
978-1-68503-036-0 $75.00

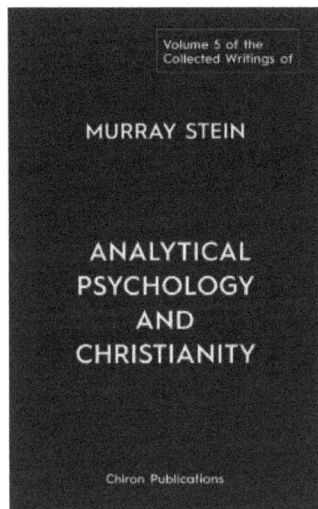

Volume 5
Analytical Psychology and Christianity

In this volume, Murray Stein illuminates Jung's relationship with Christianity and how he strove to restore its transcendent symbols.

Paperback
978-1-68503-137-4 $37.00
Hardcover
978-1-68503-138-1 $75.00

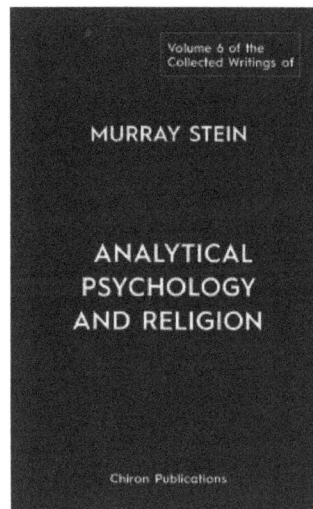

Volume 6
Analytical Psychology and Religion

This volume continues where Volume 5 left off- the archetypal exploration of religion in general and Christianity in particular, asking what it might look like if we interpreted the Christian Bible as if it were a dream.

Paperback
978-1-68503-084-1 $37.00
Hardcover
978-1-68503-085-8 $75.00

DSM-5-TR Insanely Simplified: Unlocking the Spectrums within DSM-5-TR and ICD-10

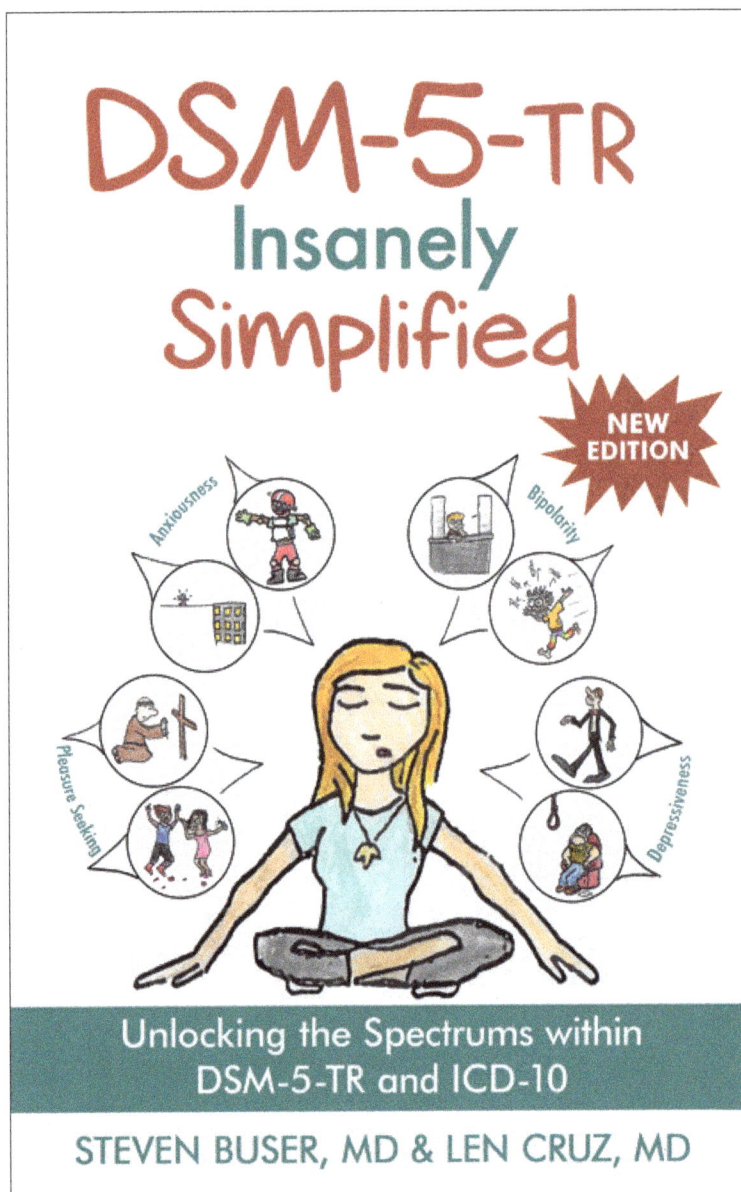

The publication of the Diagnostic and Statistical Manual Version 5 (DSM-5, 2013) and the more recent Diagnostic and Statistical Manual Version 5 – Text Revision edition (DSM-5-TR, 2022), together ushered in a major change to the field of mental health diagnosis. *DSM-5-TR Insanely Simplified* provides a summary of key concepts of the new diagnostic schema introduced in DSM-5 as well as the updated DSM-5-TR. It utilizes a variety of techniques to help clinicians master the new spectrum approach to diagnosis and its complex criteria.

Cartoons, mnemonic devices, and summary tables allow clinicians and students to quickly grasp and retain broad concepts and subtle nuances related to psychiatric diagnosis. *DSM-5-TR Insanely Simplified* fosters quick mastery of the most important concepts introduced in DSM-5 and continued in DSM-5-TR, while offering an entirely new way of looking at mental health along a continuum. This new approach goes beyond simply "labeling" clients with various diagnoses, but rather places them along spectrums that range from normal to problematic symptoms. Mental health professionals and laypeople will appreciate the synthesis of deep psychology and modern approaches to the diagnosis of mental illness.

Paperback 978-1-68503-044-5 $24.95
Hardcover 978-1-68503-045-2 $34.95

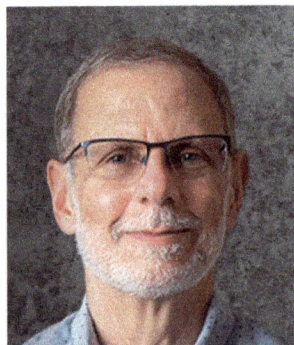

Jung's Red Book for Our Time: Searching for Soul In the 21st Century

The essays in the series are geared to the recognition that the posthumous publication of *The Red Book: Liber Novus* by C.G. Jung in 2009 was a meaningful gift to our contemporary world.

"To give birth to the ancient in a new time is creation," Jung inscribed in his *Red Book*. It is significant that this long sequestered work was published during a period in human history marked by disruption, cultural disintegration, broken boundaries, and acute anxiety.

Volume 5, the final volume in the series, contains essays that were delivered at the Eranos Symposium on "Jung's Red Book for Our Time: Searching for Soul in the 21st Century," held at Monté Veritá Conference Center in Ascona, Switzerland in 2022.

For a full list of contributors by volume, please visit our website.

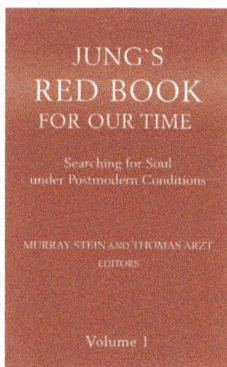

Volume 1
Paperback
978-1-63051-477-8 $37.00
Hardcover
978-1-63051-478-5 $75.00

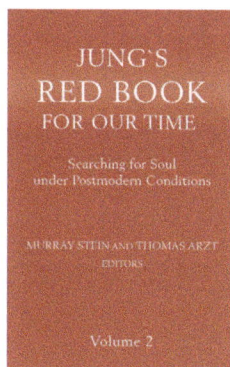

Volume 2
Paperback
978-1-63051-578-2 $37.00
Hardcover
978-1-63051-579-9 $75.00

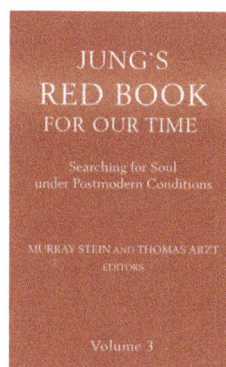

Volume 3
Paperback
978-1-63051-716-8 $37.00
Hardcover
978-1-63051-717-5 $75.00

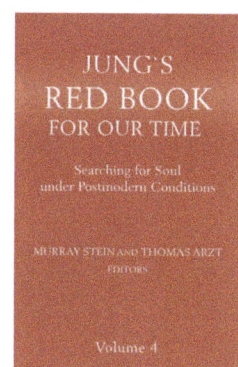

Volume 4
Paperback
978-1-63051-816-5 $37.00
Hardcover
978-1-63051-817-2 $75.00

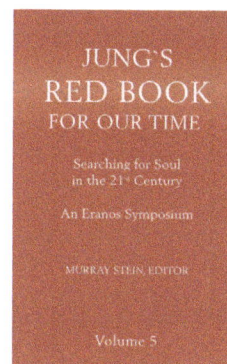

Volume 5
Paperback
978-1-68503-117-6 $37.00
Hardcover
978-1-68503-118-3 $75.00

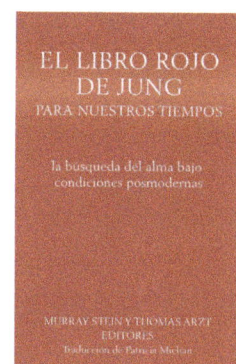

Spanish Edition
Paperback
978-1-68503-125-1 $37.00
Hardcover
978-1-68503-126-8 $75.00

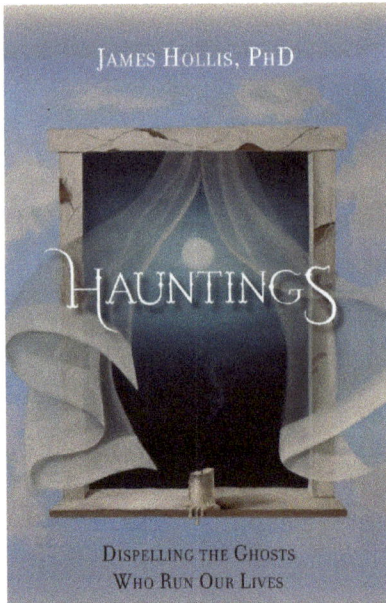

Hauntings

James Hollis considers one's transformation through the invisible world—how we are all governed by the presence of invisible forms—spirits, ghosts, ancestral and parental influences, inner voices, dreams, impulses, untold stories, complexes, synchronicities, and mysteries—which move through us, and through history. He offers a way to understand them psychologically, examining the persistence of the past in influencing our present, conscious lives and noting that engagement with mystery is what life asks of each of us. From such engagements, a deeper, more thoughtful, more considered life may come.

Paperback 978-1-63051-349-8 $21.95
Hardcover 978-1-63051-368-9 $42.00

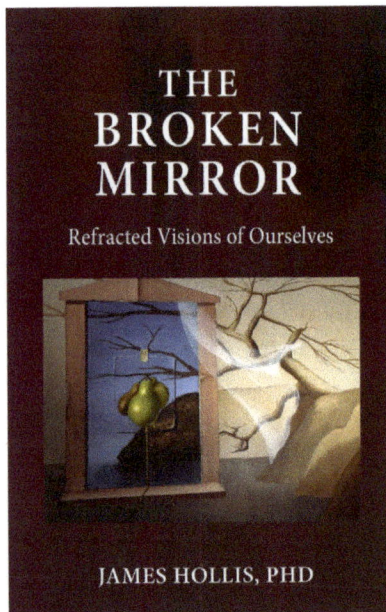

The Broken Mirror

This book explores the need to know ourselves more deeply, and the many obstacles that stand in our way. The various chapters illustrate internal obstacles such as intimidation by the magnitude of the project, the readiness to avoid the hard work, and gnawing self-doubt, but also provide tools to strengthen consciousness to take these obstacles on. Additional essays address living in haunted houses, the necessity of failure, and the gift and limits of therapy. Most of all, Hollis addresses the resources we all have within, or can obtain for ourselves, to lead a more abundant life and to step into larger possibilities for our unfolding journeys.

Paperback 978-1-68503-009-4 $24.95
Hardcover 978-1-68503-010-0 $40.00

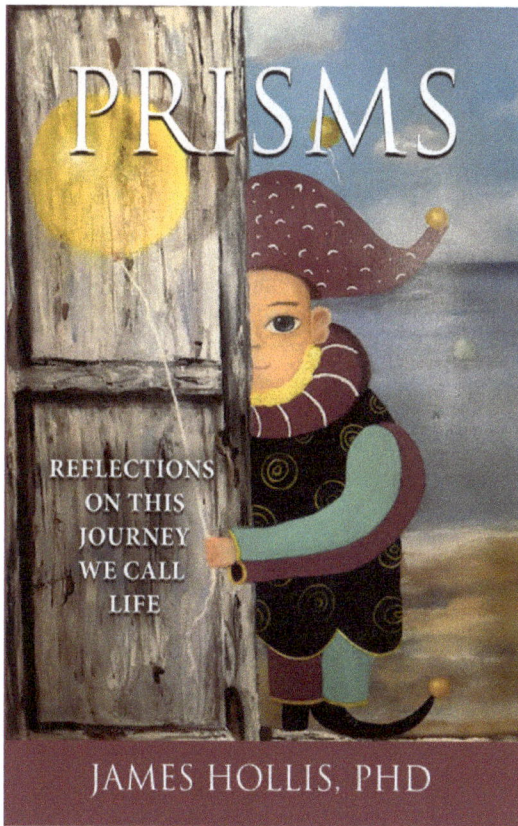

Prisms: Reflections on This Journey We Call Life

This book summarizes a lifetime of observing, engaging, and exploring why we are here, in service to what, and what life asks of us. These eleven essays, all written recently, examine how we understand ourselves, and often we have to reframe that understanding, the nature and gift of comedy, the imagination, desire, as well as our encounters with narcissism, and aging.

Paperback 978-1-63051-929-2 $26.95
Hardcover 978-1-63051-930-8 $40.00

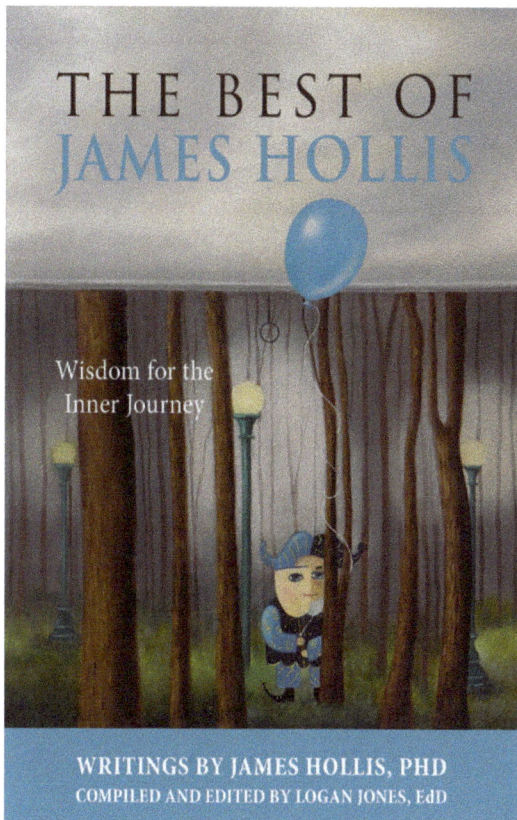

The Best of James Hollis: Wisdom for the Inner Journey

A collection of excerpts from the writings of James Hollis, these selections, compiled by editor Logan Jones, span across his body of work from *The Middle Passage* (1993) to *Prisms* (2021) and are organized into different topics ranging from the psychological concepts of Carl Jung to the everyday tasks of our living and callings.

Paperback 978-1-63051-976-6 $26.95
Hardcover 978-1-63051-977-3 $42.00

Map of the Soul Series by Murray Stein

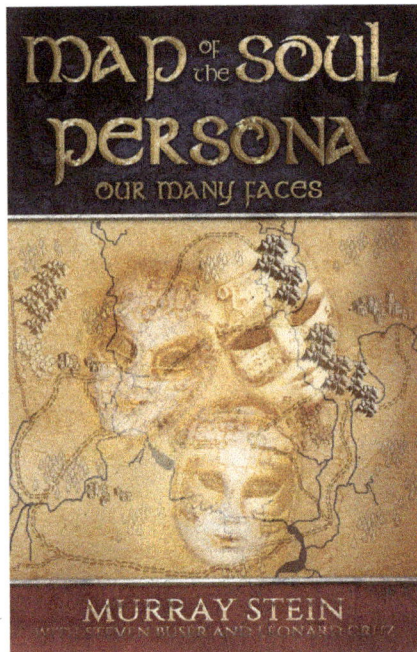

Map of the Soul – Persona
Our Many Faces

What is our persona and how does it affect our life's journey? What masks do we wear as we engage those around us? Our persona is ultimately how we relate to the world. Combined with our ego, shadow, anima and other intra-psychic elements it creates an internal map of the soul.

Paperback
978-1-63051-720-5 $14.95
Hardcover
978-1-63051-721-2 $26.95

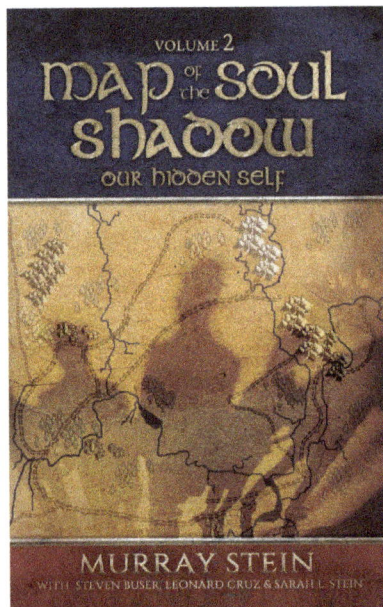

Map of the Soul – Shadow
Our Hidden Self

Dr. Murray Stein explores the dark recesses of our psyche, as well as the shadow images in BTS's latest songs in their album *Map of the Soul: 7.*

Paperback
978-1-63051-800-4 $14.95
Hardcover
978-1-63051-801-1 $26.95

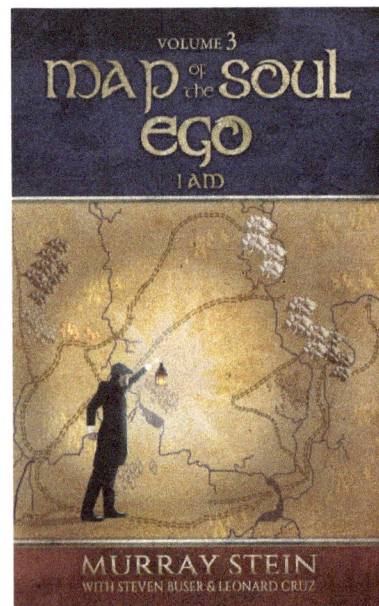

Map of the Soul – Ego
I Am

Dr. Murray Stein explores the beginnings of consciousness and the concept of the "I," as well as the evocative lyrics from the Korean Pop band BTS's album, *Map of the Soul: 7.*

Paperback
978-1-63051-841-7 $14.95
Hardcover
978-1-63051-842-4 $26.95

Map of the Soul

La Persona, l'Ombre et l'Ego dans le monde de BTS

French Edition

Paperback
978-1-63051-912-4 $16.95
Hardcover
978-1-63051-913-1 $32.00

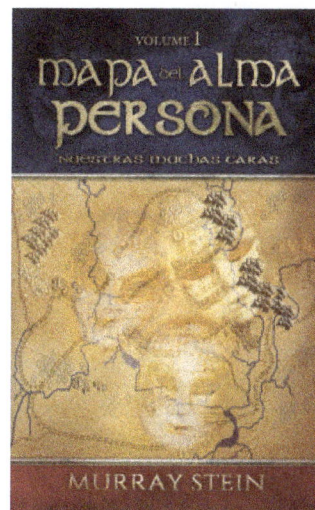

Mapa Del Alma - Persona

Nuestras Muchas Caras

Spanish Edition

Paperback
978-1-63051-788-5 $14.95
Hardcover
978-1-63051-789-2 $26.95

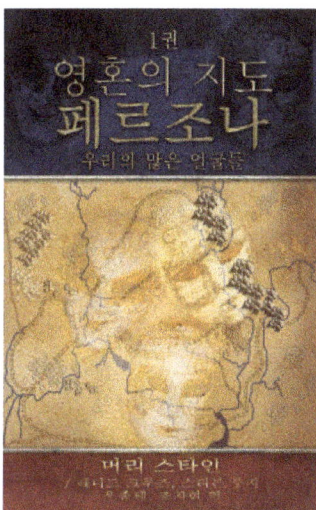

영혼의 지도: 우리의 많은 얼굴들

Korean Edition

Paperback
978-1-63051-808-0 $14.95
Hardcover
978-1-63051-809-7 $26.95

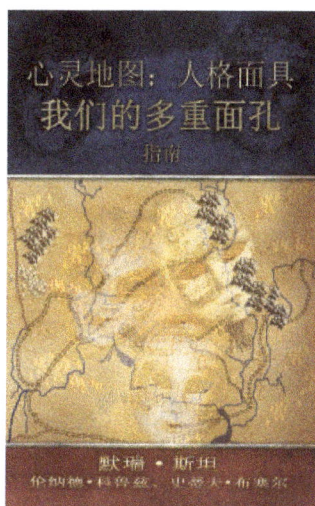

心灵地图：人格面具: 我们的多重面孔

Chinese Edition

Paperback
978-1-63051-824-0 $14.95
Hardcover
978-1-63051-825-7 $26.95

Map of the Soul 7:
Persona, Shadow & Ego in the world of BTS

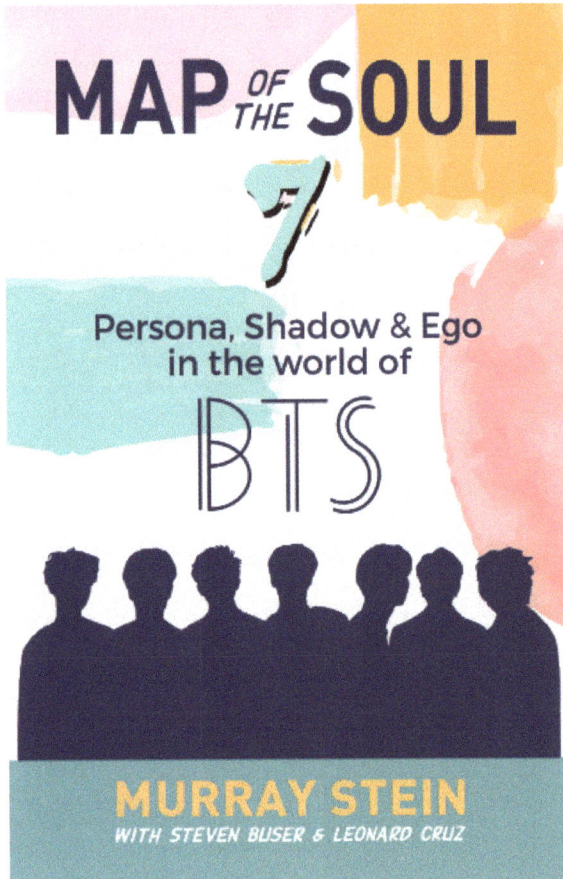

When you stand on the threshold of a new land, it is useful to have a map as your guide. The great psychologist of the 20th Century, Carl Jung, created a *Map of the Soul* that many people in his time found more than a little helpful, even lifesaving. It is even more so now, for people in the 21st Century caught in the profound complexities of modern life. Equipped with this map, individuals can navigate through life's journey with greater success. This book aims to present this map as clearly as possible.

BTS, the Korean K-pop band, is widely considered the world's most popular band. Fans of BTS have been struck by the profound depth of meaning in the songs featured in their recent album, *Map of the Soul: 7*. These songs encourage listeners to reflect deeply on the nature of ambition, the perils of worldly success, and the human spirit's resilience to overcome challenges. They serve as a guide for individuals embarking on life's journey, particularly in navigating challenging relationships. The songs are reflective, offering a mirror to our struggles to become and flourish.

Map of the Soul 7: Persona, Shadow & Ego in the World of BTS is a book that not only presents an internal map of our souls but does so within the context of a BTS album that is transforming the lives of millions of young people. It serves as a compass for those venturing into new lands.

Paperback
978-1-63051-850-9 $16.95
Hardcover
978-1-63051-851-6 $32.00

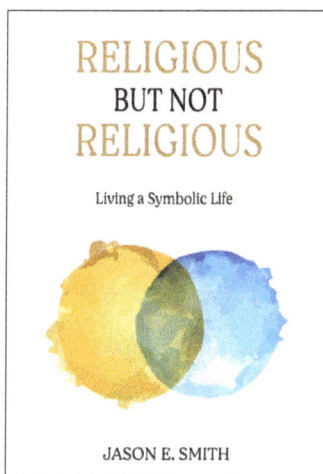

Religious But Not Religious: Living a Symbolic Life

In *Religious but Not Religious*, Jungian analyst Jason E. Smith explores the idea, expressed by C. G. Jung, that the religious sense is a natural and vital function of the human psyche. We suffer from its lack. The symbolic forms of religion mediate unconscious and ineffable experiences to the field of consciousness that infuse our lives with meaning and purpose. That is why we cannot be indifferent toward the decline of traditional religious observance so widely discussed today. The great religions house the accumulated spiritual wisdom of humankind, and their loss would be catastrophic to the human soul.

Paperback 978-1-63051-899-8 $21.95
Hardcover 978-1-63051-900-1 $32.00

Susan Rowland's Mary Wandwalker Mystery Series

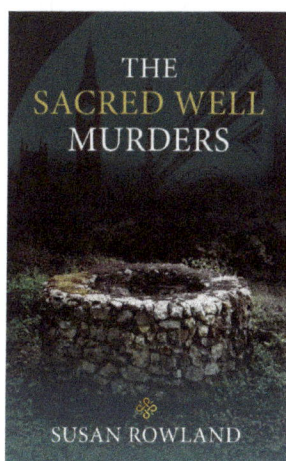

The Sacred Well Murders

A simple job turns deadly when Mary Wandwalker, novice detective, is hired to chaperone a young American, Rhiannon, to the Oxford University Summer School on the ancient Celts. Worried by a rhetoric of blood sacrifice, Mary and her operatives, Caroline, and Anna, attend a sacrifice at a sacred well. They discover that those who fail to individuate their gods become possessed by them.

Paperback
978-1-68503-005-6 $16.95
Hardcover
978-1-68503-006-3 $32.00

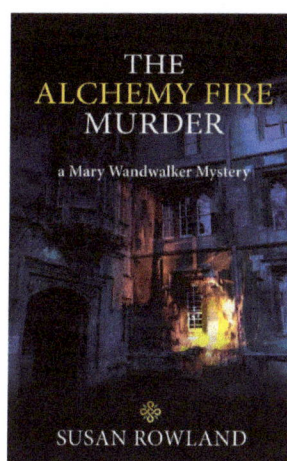

The Alchemy Fire Murder

Former Archivist Mary Wandwalker hates bringing bad news. Nevertheless, she confirms to her alma mater that their prized medieval alchemy scroll, is, in fact, a seventeenth century copy. She learns that the original vanished to colonial Connecticut with alchemist, Robert Le More. Later the genuine scroll surfaces in Los Angeles. Given that the authentic artifact is needed for her Oxford college to survive, retrieving it is essential.

Paperback
978-1-68503-129-9 $19.95
Hardcover
978-1-68503-130-5 $37.00

Inner Gold – Understanding Psychological Projection

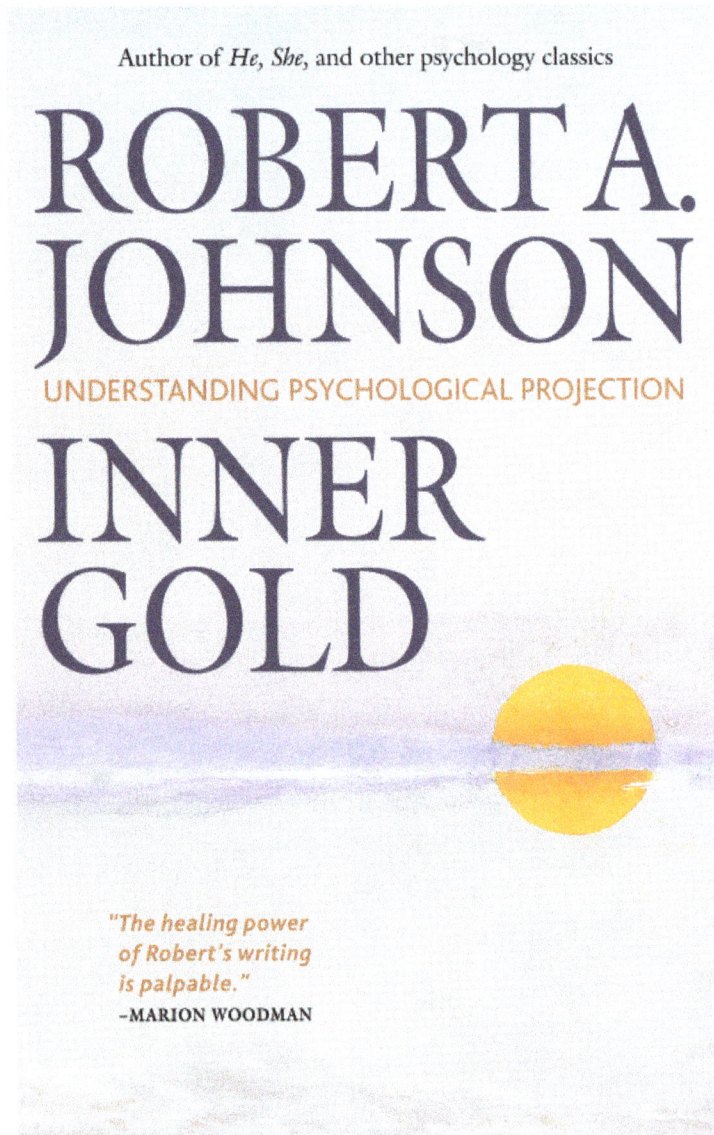

Author of *He, She,* and other psychology classics

ROBERT A. JOHNSON

UNDERSTANDING PSYCHOLOGICAL PROJECTION

INNER GOLD

"The healing power of Robert's writing is palpable."
—MARION WOODMAN

Robert A. Johnson, bestselling author of *He, She, We,* and other psychology classics, shares a lifetime of insights and experiences in this easy-to-read explanation of psychological projection — seeing unacceptable traits in others that are actually within us. Drawing on early Christianity, medieval alchemy, depth psychology, and the myths of "The Flying Dutchman" and "The Once and Future King," he also explores the subjects of loneliness, fundamentalist religion, and the spiritual dimensions of psychology.

One of the most influential and visionary analysts of his generation, Johnson follows the tradition of Carl Jung and Joseph Campbell whose ideas shed light upon our deepest metaphors of self and psyche. Johnson's books are known for presenting Jung's complex theories with simplicity and grace.

With twinkling eyes and the smile of a wise old man, Robert Johnson brings us the wisdom of a life fully lived….The healing power of Robert's writing is palpable.

  - Marion Woodman

Robert Johnson's work always has that naked intensity that tells you you're in the psychic house of an honest man.

  - Robert Bly

Available in Paperback Only
978-0-98216-566-9 $19.95

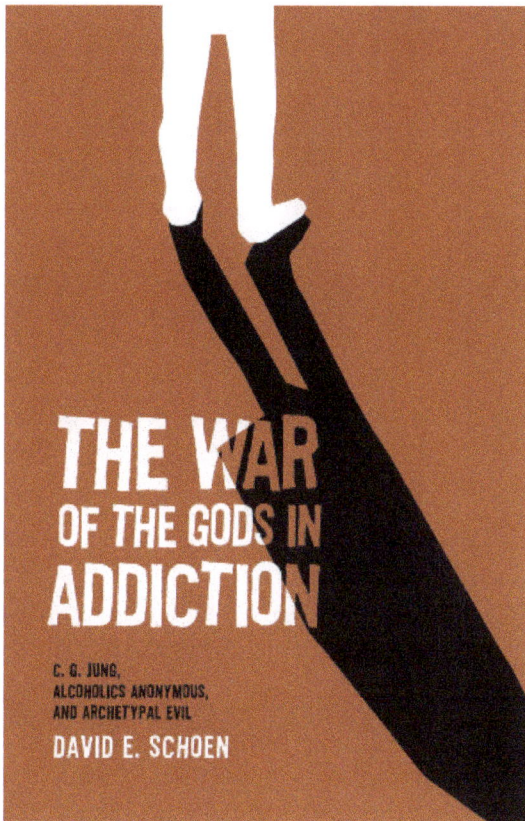

The War of the Gods in Addiction

C.G. Jung, Alcoholics Anonymous, and Archetypal Evil

The War of the Gods of Addiction, based on the correspondence between Bill W., one of the founders of Alcoholics Anonymous, and Swiss psychiatrist, C.G. Jung, proposes an original, groundbreaking, psychodynamic view of addiction. Using insights from Jungian psychology, it demonstrates why the twelve steps of AA really work.

Paperback
978-1-63051-920-9 $21.95
Hardcover
978-1-63051-921-6 $32.00

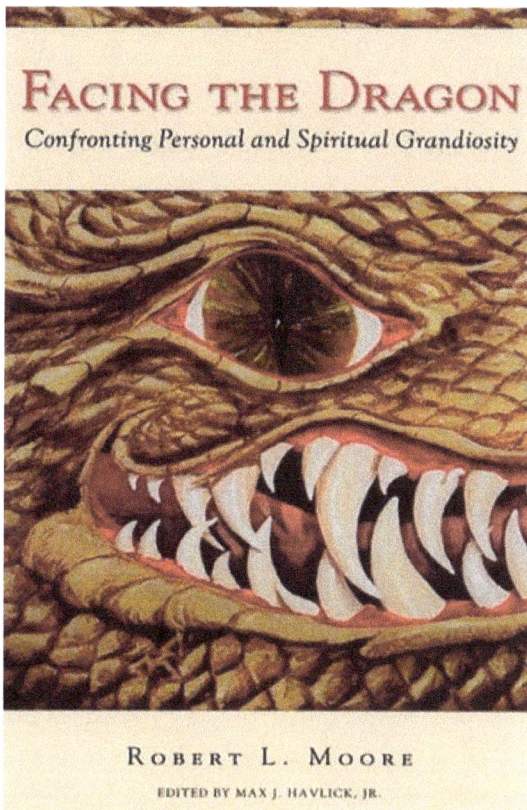

Facing the Dragon

Confronting Personal and Spiritual Grandiosity

Structured around a series of lectures presented at the Jung Institute of Chicago in a program entitled "Jungian Psychology and Human Spirituality: Liberation from Tribalism in Religious Life," this book-length essay attacks the related problems of human evil, spiritual narcissism, secularism and ritual, and grandiosity. Robert Moore dares to insist that we stop ignoring these issues and provides clear-sighted guidance for where to start and what to expect. Along the way, he pulls together many important threads from recent findings in theology, spirituality, and psychology and brings us to a point where we can conceive of embarking on a corrective course.

Paperback
978-1-888602-21-0 $21.95
Hardcover
978-1-63051-040-4 $42.00

The Barbara Hannah Collection

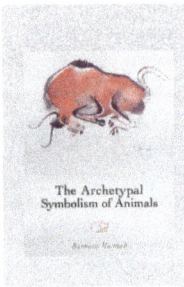

Archetypal Symbolism of Animals

Barbara Hannah, a student and a close friend of C.G. Jung, presents lectures on the symbolic meaning of several domestic and wild animals.

Paperback
978-1-63051-074-9 $32.00
Hardcover
978-1-63051-049-7 $44.95

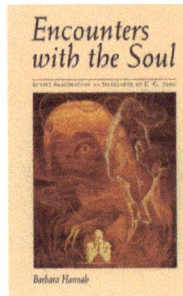

Encounters with the Soul

Barbara Hannah explores Jung's method of "active imagination" and traces the human journey toward personal wholeness.

Paperback
978-1-63051-350-4 $28.00
Hardcover
978-1-63051-034-3 $65.00

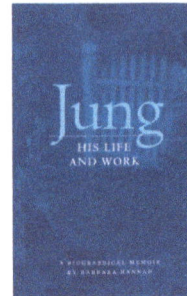

Jung: His Life and Work

Published originally in 1976, this work has become a classic retelling of Jung's life and work by one of his most dedicated followers and intimate friends. Now back in print, this work deserves to occupy a place of importance in every Jungian library.

Paperback
978-1-88860-207-4 $28.00
Hardcover
978-1-63051-031-2 $65.00

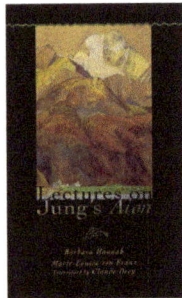

Lectures on Jung's Aion

Aion, a major work from Jung's later years, has long been a source of fascination for a wide variety of scholars and thinkers. Presented here are two substantial commentaries concerning this rich and complex text by two important figures in Jung's life and work: Barbara Hannah and Marie-Louise von Franz.

Paperback
978-1-63051-347-4 $28.00
Hardcover
978-1-63051-045-9 $65.00

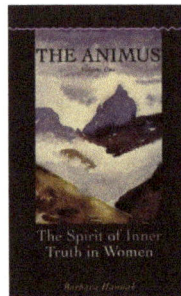

The Animus Volume 1

This volume presents Barbara Hannah's psychological analysis of the animus, which she tackled with a comprehensiveness unsurpassed in Jungian literature.

Paperback
978-1-888602-46-3 $32.00
Hardcover
978-1-63051-060-2 $44.95

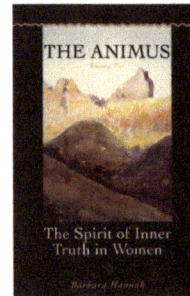

The Animus Volume 2

Volume 2 in Barbara Hannah's psychological analysis of the animus, which she tackled with a comprehensiveness unsurpassed in Jungian literature.

Paperback
978-1-88860-247-0 $32.00
Hardcover
978-1-63051-061-9 $44.95

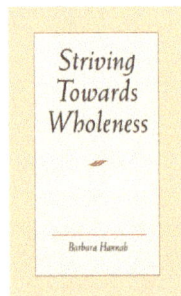

Striving Toward Wholeness

Barbara Hannah studies the psychic processes that move people to strive for wholeness of personality, an integration of all innate capacities.

Paperback 978-1-88860-213-5 $27.95
Hardcover 978-1-63051-036-7 $44.00

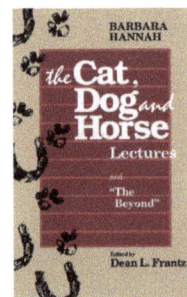

The Cat, Dog, Horse Lectures and "The Beyond"

This book features a seminar Barbara Hannah gave at the Psychological Club in 1954 about the images of the cat, the dog, and the horse in the psychological and cultural life of the western world.

Paperback 978-0-93302-959-0 $21.95
Hardcover 978-1-63051-000-8 $42.00

The Lionel Corbett Collection

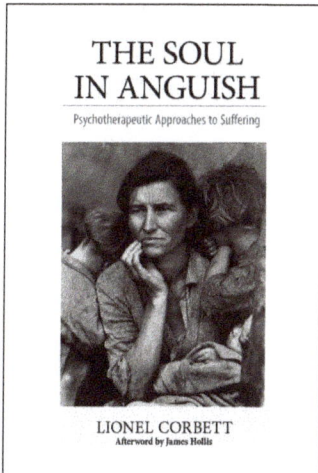

The Soul in Anguish

Psychotherapeutic Approaches to Suffering

The Soul in Anguish presents a variety of approaches to psycho-therapeutic work with suffering people, from the perspectives of both Jungian and psychoanalytic psychology. An important theme of the book is the impact of suffering—suffering may be harmful or helpful to the development of the personality. Our culture tends to assume that suffering is invariably negative or pointless, but this is not necessarily so; suffering may be destructive, but it may lead to positive developments such as enhanced empathy for others, wisdom, or spiritual development.

Paperback 978-1-63051-235-4 $28.00
Hardcover 978-1-63051-236-1 $65.00

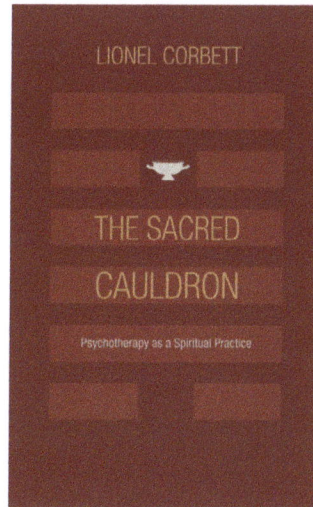

The Sacred Cauldron

Psychotherapy as a Spiritual Practice

At a time when psy-chotherapy seems to be a purely secular pursuit with no connection to the sacred, *The Sacred Cauldron* makes the startling claim that, for both participants, psycho-therapeutic work is actually a spiritual discipline in its own right. The psyche manifests the sacred and provides the transpersonal field within which the work of therapy is carried out. This book demonstrates some of the ways in which a spiritual sensibility can inform the technical aspects of psychotherapy.

Paperback 978-1-63051-275-0 $24.95
Hardcover 978-1-88860-265-4 $37.95

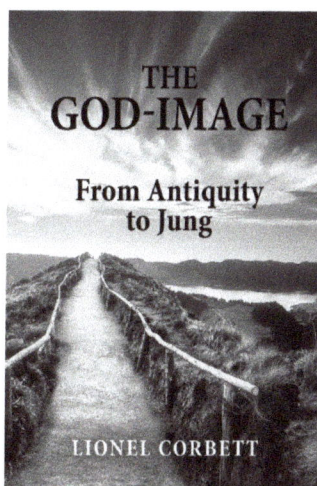

The God-image

From Antiquity to Jung

This book describes the development of images of God, beginning in antiquity and culminating in Jung's notion of the Self, an image of God in the psyche that Jung calls the God within. Over the course of history, the Self has been projected onto many local gods and goddesses and given different names and attributes. These deities are typically imagined as existing in a heavenly realm, but Jung's approach recalls them to their origins in the objective psyche.

Paperback
978-1-63051-984-1 $34.00
Hardcover
978-1-63051-985-8 $49.00

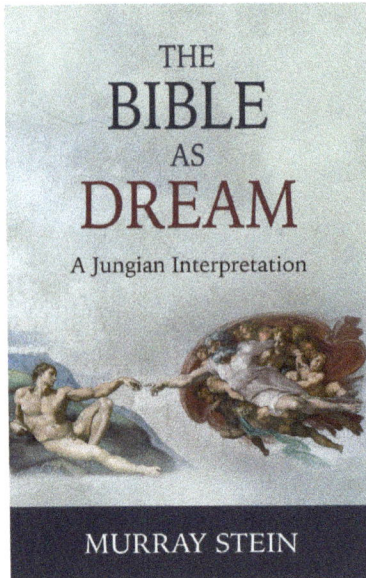

The Bible as Dream
A Jungian Interpretation

Recognized as a winner in the Applied Category of the American Board & Academy of Psychoanalysis' 2019 Book Awards. Murray Stein shares these timeless lectures—a work of respectful and loving interpretation. The Bible presents a world elaborated with reference to a specific God image. The biblical world is the visionary product of a particular people, the ancient Hebrews and the early Christians, who delved deeply into their God image and pulled from it the multitude of perspectives, rules for life, spiritual practices, and practical implications that all together created the tapestry that we find depicted in the canonical Bible.

Paperback 978-1-63051-668-0 $26.95
Hardcover 978-1-63051-669-7 $47.00

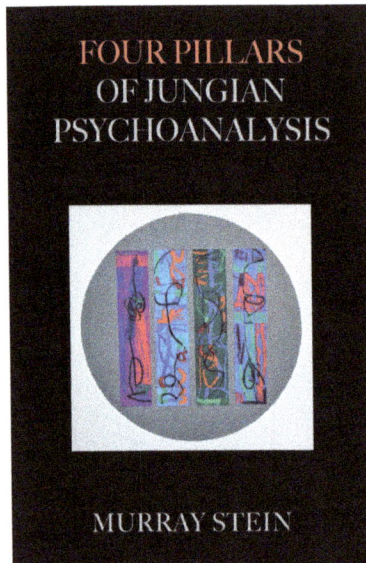

Four Pillars of Jungian Psychoanalysis

*The Four Pillars of Jungian Psychoanalysi*s by Murray Stein is a work that describes the methods that in combination sets this form of psychotherapy apart from all the others. The first chapter describes how the theory of individuation serves as an assessment tool for the analyst and guides the process toward the client's further psychological development. The second chapter, on the analytic relationship, discusses the depth psychological understanding of the healing effect of the therapeutic encounter.

Paperback 978-1-68503-025-4 $27.00
Hardcover 978-1-68503-026-1 $39.00

©2023 Chiron Publications | www.chironpublications.com

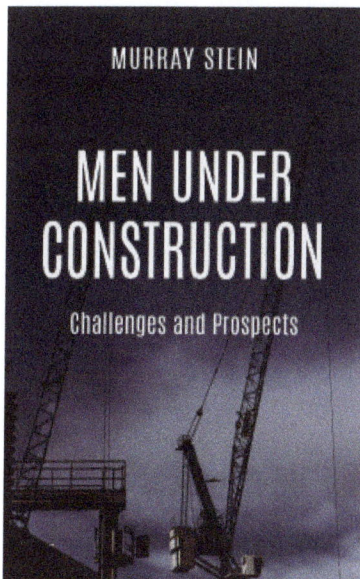

Men Under Construction
Challenges and Prospects

Today more than ever men are challenged to take steps toward greater consciousness and psychological development. In these lectures Murray Stein describes five "eras" or stages in a lifelong process of psychological and spiritual growth, as well as speaking about friendship between men and the archetypal gestures of fathering. The lectures are intended to help men of all ages to orient themselves in their lives as they search for meaning and seek personal development.

Paperback 978-1-63051-792-2 $26.95
Hardcover 978-1-63051-793-9 $47.00

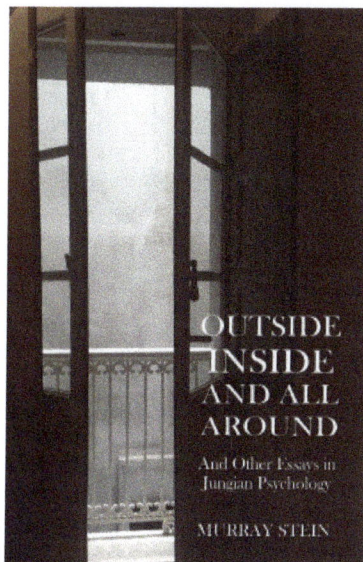

Outside Inside and All Around
And Other Essays in Jungian Psychology

In these late essays, Murray Stein circles around familiar Jungian themes such as synchronicity, individuation, archetypal image and symbol with a view to bringing these ideas into today's largely globalized cultural space.

Paperback 978-1-63051-426-6 $32.00
Hardcover 978-1-63051-427-3 $75.00

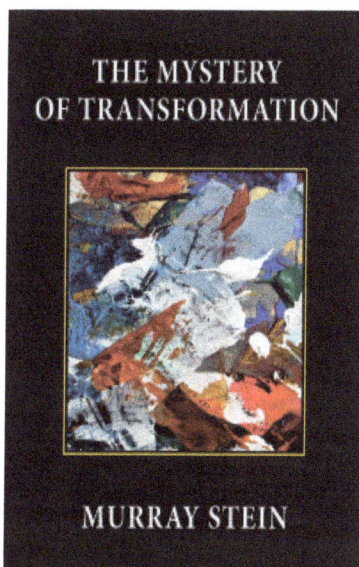

The Mystery of Transformation

This work consists of a series of probes into the mystery of the individuation process. Central to the discussion are Jung's late writings on the alchemy of psychological transformation in the late stages of individuation.

Paperback 978-1-68503-068-1 $29.00
Hardcover 978-1-68503-069-8 $42.00

The Murray Stein Collection

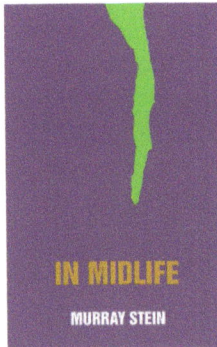

In Midlife
A Jungian Perspective

Murray Stein

Midlife: crisis, anger, change… Drawing on analytic experience, dreams, and myths, Murray Stein, a well-known analyst, formulates the three main features of the middle passage.

Paperback 978-1-63051-089-3 $24.95
Hardcover 978-1-63051-090-9 $65

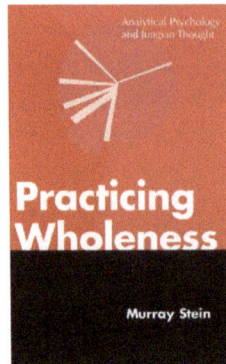

Practicing Wholeness

Murray Stein

Murray Stein argues that practicing wholeness is relevant to many areas of our lives: our private inner worlds; our religious beliefs, images, and rituals; our organizational involvements; and our cultural paradigms.

Paperback 978-1-63051-091-6 $21.95
Hardcover 978-1-63051-092-3 $42

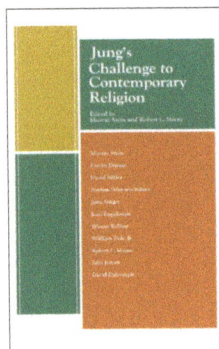

Jung's Challenge to Contemporary Religion

Murray Stein and Robert Moore

Highlights of this book include studies of the way in which Christianity is changing, the feminine dimension of God, and Jung's contribution to biblical humanities.

Paperback 978-1-63051-253-8 $26.95
Hardcover 978-1-88860-276-0 $42

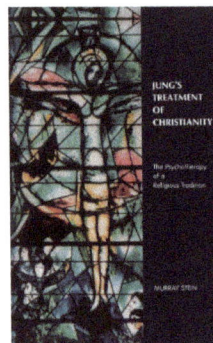

Jung's Treatment of Christianity
The Psychotherapy of a Religious Tradition

Murray Stein

An insightful and convincing interpretation of Jung's encounter with Christianity. Murray Stein provides a comprehensive analysis of Jung's writings on Christianity in relation to his personal life, psychological thought, and efforts to transform Western religion.

Paperback 978-1-63051-267-5 $28
Hardcover 978-1-88860-268-5 $65

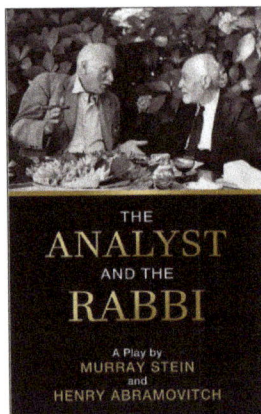

The Analyst and the Rabbi

Murray Stein and Henry Abramovitch

A meeting between C.G. Jung and Rabbi Leo Baeck took place in Zurich in October 1946 at the Savoy Hotel Baur en Ville. Very little is actually known about this meeting. This play is an imaginative construction of what might have happened in this historic meeting of two great men.

Paperback
978-1-63051-732-8 $19.95
Hardcover
978-1-63051-733-5 $29.95

©2023 Chiron Publications | www.chironpublications.com

Murray Stein and
Lionel Corbett

Psyche's Stories Volume 1
Modern Jungian Interpretations of Fairy Tales

Fairy tales can reveal a hidden side of our lives, our unconscious, and our interrelationship with others. Each of these essays provides a Jungian interpretation of a well-known or rare fairy tale to reveal the universal psychic dynamics that affect us in our lives and collectively in the world around us. In this volume, *Allerleirauh, Beauty and the Beast, The Wonderful Sheep, Cinderella, Cupid and Psyche, The Devil's Sooty Brother, The Fisherman and His Wife, Fitcher's Bird* and *The Goose Girl* are examined.

Paperback 978-1-63051-265-1 $27.95
Hardcover 978-1-88860-298-2 $65

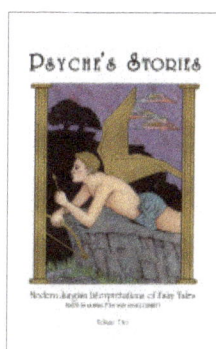

Murray Stein and
Lionel Corbett

Psyche's Stories
Volume 2
Modern Jungian Interpretations of Fairy Tales

In this volume, *Maid Maleen, The Old Woman in the Wood, Oisin's Mother, Rapunzel, The Snow Queen, Sunahsepa and Akanandun, The Water of Life, The White Snake, Snow White, Cinderella and Dracula* are examined.

Paperback 978-0-93302-956-9 $26.95
Hardcover 978-1-63051-006-0 $65

Murray Stein and
Lionel Corbett

Psyche's Stories
Volume 3
Modern Jungian Interpretations of Fairy Tales

In this volume, *The White Snake, Clever Elsie, The Girl Without Hands, Snow White, Cinderella, Pinocchio, The Tsar, His Son,* and the *Swan Princess* are examined.

Paperback 978-0-93302-990-3 $26.95
Hardcover 978-1-63051-017-6 $37.95

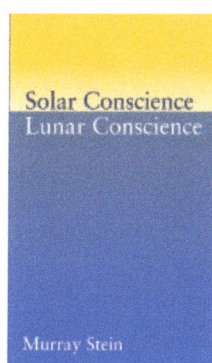

Murray Stein

Solar Conscience/Lunar Conscience
The Psychological Foundations of Morality, Lawfulness, and the Sense of Justice

Murray Stein explores the origins and work of conscience. Using the myths of Orestes and Prometheus as examples, he defines solar conscience as an inner voice that represents the values of society, and lunar conscience as an instinctive inner sense which seeks to fulfill underlying qualities of right and wrong.

Paperback 978-1-63051-268-2 $21.95
Hardcover 978-1-63051-011-4 $32

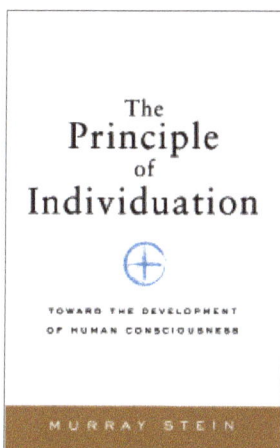

Murray Stein

The Principle of Individuation
Toward the Development of Human Consciousness

The Principle of Individuation suggests new approaches, on both personal and communal levels, for gaining freedom from the compulsion to repeat endlessly the dysfunctional patterns that have conditioned us. In this concise and contemporary account of the process of individuation, Murray Stein sets out its two basic movements and then examines the central role of numinous experience, the critical importance of initiation, and the unique psychic space required for its unfolding.

Paperback
978-163051-264-4 $28
Hardcover
978-1-63051-053-4 $65

The Zürich Lecture Series

The Zürich Lecture Series in Analytical Psychology is hosted by the International School of Analytical Psychology Zürich (ISAPZURICH) and Chiron Publications to present annually new work by a distinguished scholar who has previously offered innovative contributions to the field of Analytical Psychology by either:

- bringing analytical psychology into meaningful dialogue with other scientific, artistic, and academic disciplines
- showing how analytical psychology can lead to a better understanding of contemporary global concerns relating to the environment, politics, religion
- expanding the concepts of analytical psychology as they are applied clinically

Each year, the selected lecturer delivers lectures in Zürich based on a previously unpublished book-length work. This book is then published by Chiron Publications. Murray Stein, Leonard Cruz and Steven Buser are the Series Editors.

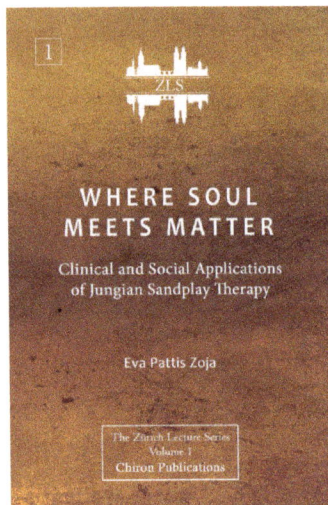

Volume 1
Where Soul Meets Matter
Clinical and Social Applications of Jungian Sandplay Therapy
by Eva Pattis

The author explores the psyche's astonishing capacity and determination to regulate itself by creating images and narratives as soon as a free and protected space for expression is provided. A variety of examples from analytic practice with adults and from psychosocial projects with children in vulnerable situations illustrate how sandplay can be used in different therapeutic settings.

182 Pages
Paperback 978-1-63051-752-6 $27
Hardcover 978-1-63051-753-3 $42

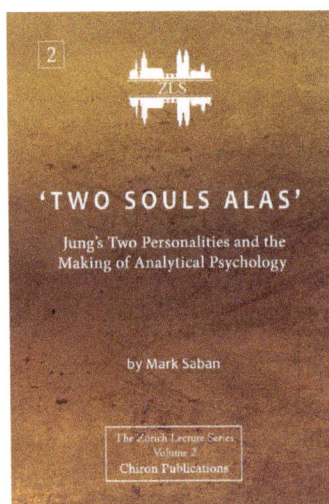

Volume 2
'Two Souls Alas'
Jung's Two Personalities and the Making of Analytical Psychology
by Mark Saban

This is the first book to suggest that Jung's experience of the difficult dynamic between these two personalities not only informs basic principles behind the development of Jung's psychological model but underscores the theory and practice of Analytical Psychology as a whole.

264 Pages
Paperback 978-1-63051-748-9 $29
Hardcover 978-1-63051-749-6 $42

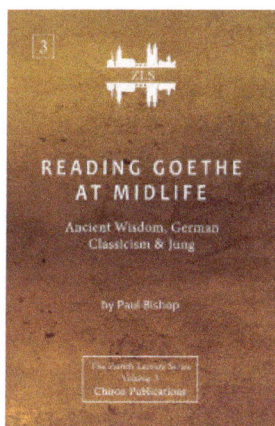

Volume 3
Reading Goethe at Midlife
Ancient Wisdom, German Classicism & Jung
by Paul Bishop

This book reveals the remarkable symmetry between the ideas and Jung and Goethe. Jung's analysis of the stages of life, and his advice to heed the "call of the self," are brought into the conjunction with Goethe's emphasis on the importance of hope, showing an underlying continuity of thought and relevance from ancient wisdom, via German classicism to analytical psychology.

302 Pages
Paperback 978-1-63051-828-8 $29
Hardcover 978-1-63051-829-5 $42

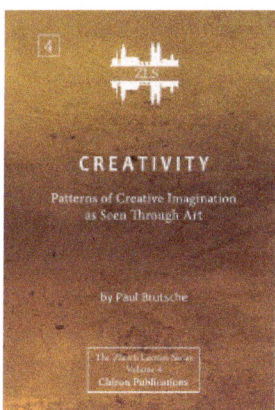

Volume 4
Creativity
Patterns of Creative Imagination as Seen Through Art
by Paul Brutsche

We don't know where creativity comes from. This book does not claim to reveal this secret. It does not attempt to reduce creativity to a "nothing but," for example to explain it as a special ability of certain creative individuals with special abilities. On the contrary, it is about exploring the fullness and variety of this amazing power, which is the basis of all cultural, artistic, scientific and spiritual activity of man, without attributing it to a simple cause.

316 Pages
Paperback 978-1-63051-883-7 $32
Hardcover 978-1-63051-884-4 $49

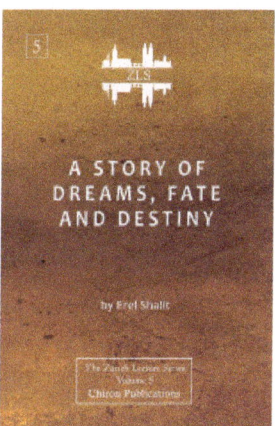

Volume 5
A Story of Dreams, Fate and Destiny
by Erel Shalit

Erel Shalit "calls attention to the dream and its images along the nocturnal axis that leads us from fate to destiny."

202 Pages
Paperback 978-1-63051-812-7 $29
Hardcover 978-1-63051-813-4 $42

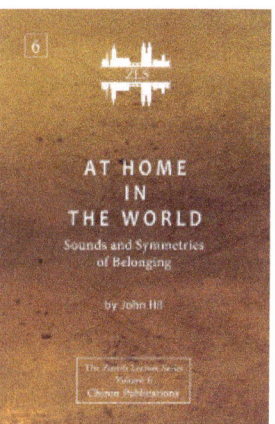

Volume 6
At Home in the World
Sounds and Symmetries of Belonging
by John Hill

Part of the Zurich Lecture Series and previously published by Spring Journal, this work offers a profound philosophical and psychological exploration of the multi-dimensional significance of home and the interwoven themes of homelessness and homesickness and contemporary global culture.

300 Pages
Paperback 978-1-68503-032-2 $29
Hardcover 978-1-68503-033-9 $42

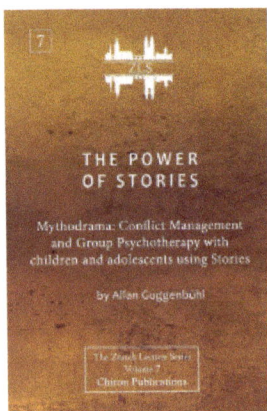

Volume 7
The Power of Stories
Mythodrama: Conflict Management and Group Psychotherapy with Children and Adolescents Using Stories

Mythodramas main focus are specially selected stories, which mirror the issues of the respective group, connect to the issues of the group, and serve as an entrance to the imaginal. This book describes how the stories are selected, told, enacted, and linked to the issues and concerns of the group or individual.

186 Pages
Paperback 978-1-68503-145-9 $29.00
Hardcover 978-1-68503-146-6 $42.00

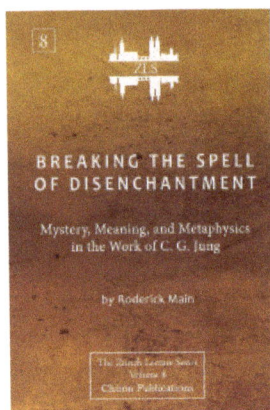

Volume 8
Breaking the Spell of Disenchantment
Mystery, Meaning, and Metaphysics in the Work of C.G. Jung
by Roderick Main

One of the most powerful narratives gripping scientists, intellectuals, and the general culture in Europe during the early decades of the twentieth century was that the world had become disenchanted: stripped of genuine mystery, lacking inherent meaning, and unrelated to any spiritual or divine reality. Roderick Main examines various ways in which C.G. Jung's analytical psychology, developed during this same period, can be seen to challenge that dominant narrative.

172 Pages
Paperback 978-1-68503-080-3 $32
Hardcover 978-1-68503-081-0 $42

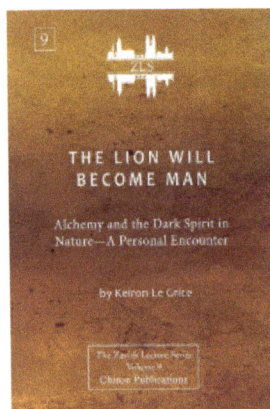

Volume 9
The Lion Will Become Man
Alchemy and the Dark Spirit in Nature—A Personal Encounter
by Keiron Le Grice

In this compelling psychological memoir, Keiron Le Grice details his experience of a profound transformative crisis between 2001 and 2004. *The Lion Will Become Man* gives a striking example of alchemy at work and reveals its great value as a guide to the complex developmental process that Jung called individuation.

Paperback 978-1-68503-157-2 $29.00
Hardcover 978-1-68503-158-9 $42.00

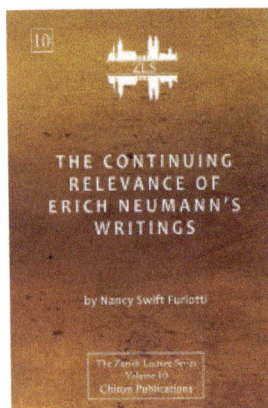

Volume 10
The Continuing Relevance of Erich Neumann's Writings
by Nancy Swift Furlotti

This book begin with an introduction to Erich Neumann, looking at who this exceptional man was, his relationship with Jung, and his move from Berlin to Palestine before WWII, then turning to examining the correspondence between Neumann and Jung, and then delve into Neumann's early writings, focusing on his work on the stages of development of consciousness, considering the results when it is successful, and what the individual and cultural implications are when it is not successful. The seeds of all Neumann's other writings and interests will be touched upon as well.

Paperback 978-1-68503-163-3 $29.00
Hardcover 978-1-68503-164-0 $42.00

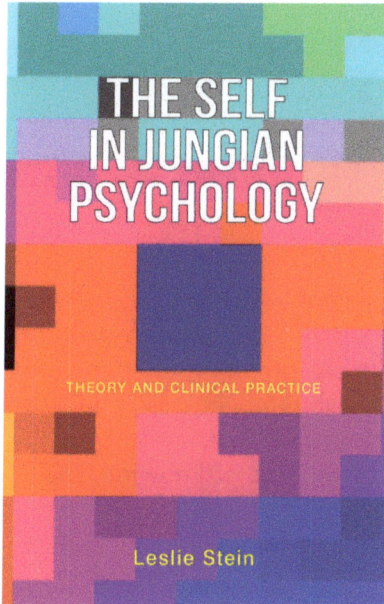

The Self in Jungian Psychology
Theory and Clinical Practice

Winner of the 2022 IAJS (International Association for Jungian Studies) Book Awards. Realizing the Self is the absolute goal of Jungian psychology. Yet as a concept it is impossibly vague as it defines a center of our being that also embraces the mystery of existence. This work synthesizes the thousands of statements Jung made about the Self in order to bring it to ground, to unravel its true purpose, and to understand how it might be able to manifest.

Paperback 978-1-63051-980-3 $34.00
Hardcover 978-1-63051-981-0 $47.00

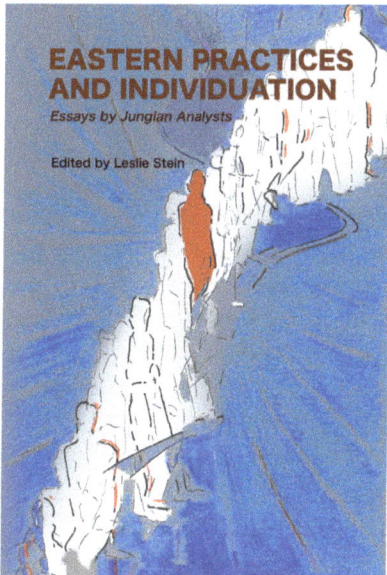

Eastern Practices and Individuation
Essays by Jungian Analysts

Edited by Leslie Stein, these essays are personal, engaging, and contain a refined analysis of whether these two paths may work together or are pointing to different end points. Contributors include: Ashok Bedi, Lionel Corbett, Royce Froehlich, Karin Jironet, Patricia Katsky, Ann Chia-Yi Li, Jim Manganiello, Judith Pickering, Leslie Stein, Murray Stein, and Polly Young-Eisendrath.

Paperback 978-1-68503-056-8 $32.00
Hardcover 978-1-68503-057-5 $45.00

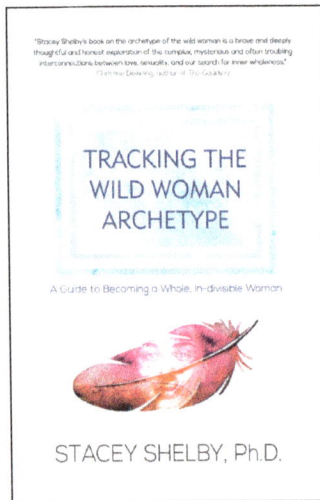

Tracking the Wild Woman Archetype
A Guide to Becoming a Whole, In-divisible Woman

Relationships can serve as the alchemical vessels of a woman's psychological transformation. *Tracking the Wild Woman Archetype* finds that the paradoxes and impossibilities of love serve to create a more profound woman who is more conscious of the manifold world of unconscious archetypes. It tracks the process of individuation and alchemical transformation through the study of texts, the author's lived experience, and imaginal ways of knowing, such as dreams, synchronicities, and active imaginations.

Paperback 978-1-63051-484-6 $21.95
Hardcover 978-1-63051-485-3 $42.00

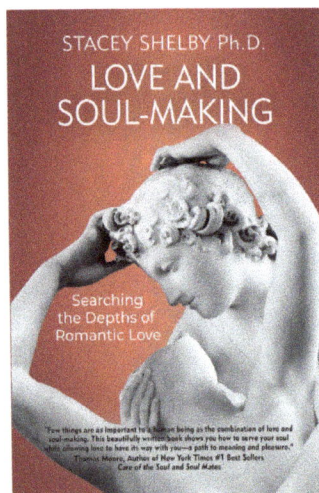

Love and Soul-Making
Searching the Depths of Romantic Love

Love and Soul-Making brings awareness to both the patriarchal origins of romance and the unarguably magical, archetypal experience of love. Relationships can serve as an alchemical vessel for the development of the soul as part of the individuation process. The struggles of relationships, whether one is partnered or not, can allow us to engage more deeply with the psyche and can guide us further into her territory. For those experiencing romantic difficulties, the myth of Psyche and Eros can serve as a guide to the stages involved in soul-making and how that is enacted in human relationships. This book encourages contemplating relationships both literally and metaphorically. With metaphorical vision, we create possibility for the alchemical transmutation process and the development of the soul. This book provides context to the soul-making process, and it can help to re-animate your creativity and vitality. Soul (Psyche) follows what she loves (Eros).

Paperback 978-1-68503-039-1 $19.95
Hardcover 978-1-68503-040-7 $37.00

Father-Daughter, Mother-Son

Freeing Ourselves from the Complexes That Bind Us

Verena Kast's *Father-Daughter, Mother-Son* was first published by Element Books in 1997. Since then, it has become a classic read for those adventuring into Carl Gustav Jung's concept of complexes—what they are, how they affect our life and shape our relationships—and for those wanting to understand more about the relationship between fathers and daughters, and mothers and sons—of whatever sex and gender.

Paperback 978-1-68503-072-8 $27.00
Hardcover 978-1-68503-073-5 $39.00

Women and Desire
Beyond Wanting to Be Wanted

Polly Young-Eisendrath´s *Women and Desire: Beyond Wanting to Be Wanted* was first published by Harmony Books in 1999. Since then, it has become a classic read for those readers—to use a cinematographic expression—who want to use analytical psychology to shed light on what women want. This book, when first published, was described (and still is) as "provocative and vital."

Paperback 978-1-68503-121-3 $30.00
Hardcover 978-1-68503-122-0 $44.00

BOOK CATEGORIES

ARTS & LITERATURE

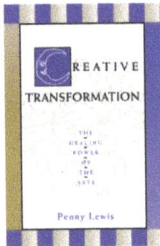

Penny Lewis
Creative Transformation
The Healing Power of the Arts

This unique account by a dance and drama therapist is the first of its kind to integrate Jungian theory, creative arts therapy, and developmental object relations theory successfully. Using the arts as a psychotherapeutic tool, trauma and addiction are explored and enacted, calling upon the imaginal realm of the arts as a vehicle for transformation and recovery.

200 Pages
Paperback
978-0-93302-966-8 $26.95
Hardcover
978-1-63051-008-4 $42

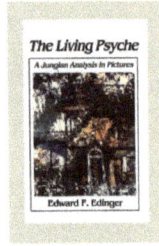

Edward F. Edinger
The Living Psyche
A Jungian Analysis in Pictures Psychotherapy

The art in this book provide a rare opportunity to experience the work of an artist and the reality of the living psyche. They touch on all the major themes of the analysis and constitute a remarkable record of an analytic experience that ranged from the heights to the depths, from the infernal to the sublime.

230 Pages
Paperback
978-1-63051-081-7 $21.95
Hardcover
978-1-88860-288-3 $65

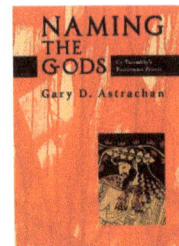

Gary D. Astrachan
Naming the Gods
Cy Twombly's Passionate Poiesis

Naming the Gods: Cy Twombly's Passionate Poiesis concerns itself with the contemporary art work of Cy Twombly and his radically innovative and necessary forms of creating for our times as seen against the deep background of classical Greek mythology.

258 Pages
Paperback
978-1-63051-736-6 $34.95
Hardcover
978-1-63051-737-3 $67

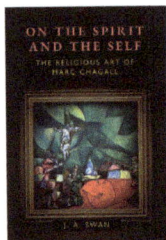

J.A. Swan
On The Spirit and The Self
The Religious Art of Marc Chagall

This book compliments and extends the scholarship surrounding Marc Chagall's place in the history of 20th century art as a religious artist. Central to this study is the psychic process of individuation and the ways in which images appear to depict the deeper changes in our collective human existence.

224 Pages
Paperback
978-1-63051-420-4 $29
Hardcover
978-1-63051-421-1 $70

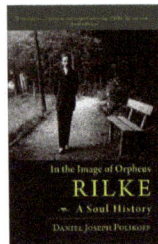

Daniel Polikoff
Rilke, A Soul History
In the Image of Orpheus

In the *Image of Orpheus* tells the inner story of Rilke's literary career, tracing—step by step—the mythopoetic journey inscribed in the interweaving lines of the poet's life and art. Blending biography with in-depth analyses of Rilke's poetry and prose (from his little-known *Visions of Christ* through the *Sonnets to Orpheus*), the lively narrative draws upon Hillman and Jung, Plato and Petrarch, Apuleius, Ibn Arabi and Lou Andreas-Salomé, as it unfolds the poet-seer's vision of the nature and destiny of the human soul—a vision as timely as it is timeless.

782 Pages
Paperback
978-1-88860-252-4 $37
Hardcover
978-1-63051-062-6 $75

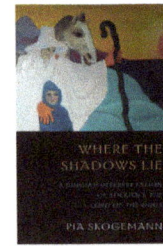

Pia Skogemann
Where the Shadows Lie
A Jungian Interpretation of Tolkien's The Lord of the Rings

Where the Shadows Lie takes the reader on a journey through Tolkien's Middle-earth, following the hobbits, their companions, and the characters they encounter on their quest. Jung's theory of the collective unconscious and the archetypes provide a key to understanding the forces of fantasy that are so powerful in Tolkien's masterpiece—and thereby a key to understanding ourselves and the events of the outside world in our modern times.

232 Pages
Paperback
978-1-88860-245-6 $18.95
Hardcover
978-1-63051-057-2 $37.95

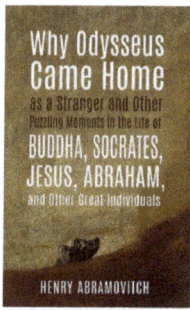

Henry Abramovitch

Why Odysseus Came Home as a Stranger and other Puzzling Moments in the Life of Buddha, Socrates, Jesus, Abraham, and other Great Individuals

Why did Socrates remember his debt to Ascalapius, the god of healing, only in his last breath? Why did Jesus, the prophet of love, curse an innocent fig tree? Why did Abraham agree to kill the son he loved the most? Why did Lot's wife look back? Why did Odysseus come home as a stranger? The short essays in this book do not try to answer these questions, but they do provide a response, enriched by Jewish tradition and Jungian psychology.

140 Pages
Paperback 978-1-63051-772-4 $27
Hardcover 978-1-63051-773-1 $37

Angelyn Spignesi

Lyrical-Analysis

The Unconscious Through Jane Eyre

A lyrical analysis of Jane Eyre and a study of literature, feminism, and psychoanalysis.

364 Pages
Paperback 978-0-93302-954-5 $21.95
Hardcover 978-1-88860-289-0 $42

Barry Ulanov

Jung and Shakespeare

Hamlet, Othello and the Tempest

Three plays analyzed from a Jungian perspective and a fresh wit, catching many contemporary nuances in these well-loved plays and their continuing relevance for today.

128 Pages
Paperback 978-1-63051-254-5 $21.95
Hardcover 978-1-63051-003-9 $42

Louise Lumen

Descent and Return

An Incest Survivor's Healing Journey Through Art Therapy

Descent and Return: An Incest Survivor's Healing Journey through Art Therapy records the progress of Jacqueline Leigh's inner journey. When Jacqueline Leigh was 38 years old, she began having spontaneous flashbacks of an incestuous childhood. This devastating experience destroyed everything she thought had been true about her life, family, and God.

256 Pages
Paperback 978-1-63051-381-8 $28
Hardcover 978-1-63051-382-5 $65

Clifton Snider

The Stuff That Dreams Are Made On

A Jungian Interpretation of Literature

In The Stuff That Dreams Are Made On: A Jungian Interpretation of Literature, Clifton Snider offers an explanation of both Jungian literary theory and Jungian psychology.

178 Pages
Paperback 978-0-93302-937-8 $21.95
Hardcover 978-1-88860-299-9 $32

BIBLICAL & OTHER SACRED LITERATURE

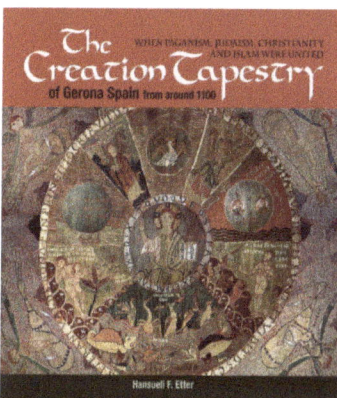

Hansueli F. Etter

The Creation Tapestry of Gerona Spain from around 1100

When Paganism, Judaism, Christianity and Islam were United

Around the year 1100 a genius mind created an image which has not lost its meaning today-the Creation Tapestry. To discover the symbolic meaning of the rich iconography of the Creation Tapestry opens up an insight in the common background of all religions back to the roots of shamanism, which use mandalas in dance as well as in images.

144 Pages
Paperback
978-1-63051-784-7 $27
Hardcover
978-1-63051-785-4 $42

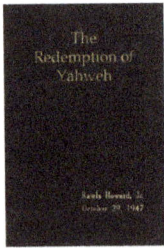

Rawls Howard, Jr.

The Redemption of Yaweh

In the darkness and primal fire of prehistory, a consciousness awakens. Gradually it takes on an identity and begins a journey, aided by a serpent companion, that lasts for millennia.

78 Pages
Paperback
978-1-63051-756-4 $16.95
Hardcover
978-1-63051-757-1 $24.95

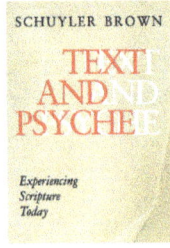

Schulyer Brown

Text and Psyche

Experiencing Scripture Today

It has been the impact of scripture upon the human heart that has changed human lives. *Text and Psyche* convincingly shows that the reader of scripture has a creative and not merely passive role.

142 Pages
Paperback
978-1-88860-223-4 $21.95
Hardcover
978-1-63051-039-8 $32

Gustav Dreifuss and Judith Riemer

Abraham, the Man and the Symbol

A Jungian Interpretation of the Biblical Story

Abraham the man was God's chosen one–chosen to impart the belief in one God to a pagan society and to bring forth a new nation in the Promised Land. Abraham the symbol shows that we all have a mission if we will heed the call from the voice of Self.

160 Pages
Paperback
978-0-93302-994-1 $21.95
Hardcover
978-1-63051-019-0 $42

BIOGRAPHY & AUTOBIOGRAPHY

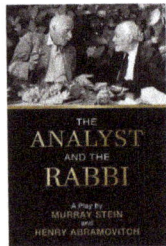

Murray Stein and Henry Abramovitch

The Analyst and the Rabbi

A meeting between C.G. Jung and Rabbi Leo Baeck took place in Zurich in October 1946 at the Savoy Hotel Baur en Ville. Very little is actually known about this meeting. This play is an imaginative construction of what might have happened in this historic meeting of two great men.

112 Pages
Paperback
978-1-63051-732-8 $19.95
Hardcover
978-1-63051-733-5 $29.95

E. A. Bennet

C.G. Jung

Thanks to E.A. Bennet's unique opportunities to hear Jung's personal perspective—on subjects from Freud to Hitler, and including a valuable correspondence about Aion, regarded as Jung's most "difficult" book—*C.G. Jung* sheds new light for today's scholars on Jung's work and on the man himself.

192 Pages
Paperback
978-1-88860-235-7 $21.95
Hardcover
978-1-63051-050-3 $50

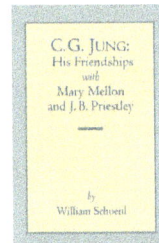

William Schoenl

C.G. Jung

His Friendships with Mary Mellon and J.B. Priestley

This story details Jung's friendships with Mary Mellon and J. B. Priestley, who both admired him and helped make his psychology known and recognized throughout the world. In this book, we get a glimpse of Jung the man, with "nose and ears," as his son Franz said of him—a remarkable genius but also a man with ordinary human strivings and flaws.

112 Pages
Paperback
978-1-88860-208-1 $14.95
Hardcover
978-1-63051-030-5 $42

Aldo Carotenuto

The Call of the Daimon

Love and Truth in the Writings of Franz Kafka

The Call of the Daimon: Love and Truth in the Writings of Franz Kafka includes Kafka's life, characters and events in the novels, contemporary poetry, and Aldo Carotenuto's interpretations of critical Jungian perspectives.

376 Pages
Available in Paperback Only
978-0-93302-983-5 $21.95

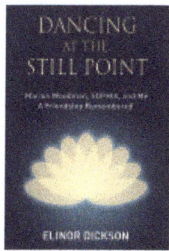

Elinor Dickson

Dancing at the Still Point

Marion Woodman, SOPHIA, and Me – A Friendship Remembered

At a time when we are witnessing the return of the World Soul, the rise of feminine consciousness and the re-enchantment of Nature, the friendship between Marion Woodman and Elinor Dickson offers us a rare glimpse into the new story yearning to be born. This book reveals a remarkable friendship rooted in Soul that is both deeply personal and transpersonal.

202 Pages
Paperback
978-1-63051-695-6 $24.95
Hardcover
978-1-63051-696-3 $39

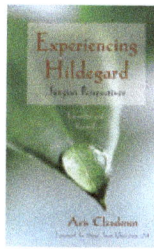

Avis Clendenen

Experiencing Hildegard

Jungian Perspectives - Expanded and Revised

This exploration of Hildegard of Bingen is a synthesis of her spirituality with Jungian depth psychology insights, the unconscious and reality of the soul.

224 Pages
Available in Paperback Only
978-1-88860-258-6 $26.95

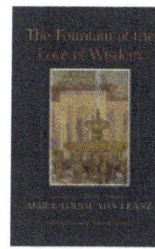

Sylvia Shaindel Senensky

The Fountain of the Love of Wisdom

A Homage to Marie Louise Von Franz

A commemorative volume in memory of Dr. Marie-Louise von Franz, who is remembered as one of the perhaps most important and beloved of Carl Jung's students.

640 Pages
Paperback
978-1-88860-238-8 $37
Hardcover
978-1-63051-052-7 $49.95

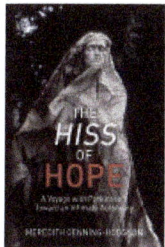

Meredith Oenning-Hodgson

The Hiss of Hope

A Voyage with Parkinson's Towards an Intimate Autonomy

The diagnosis of a chronic illness can separate a person's timeline into two spaces: the *before* and the *after* of the onset of the disease. For author Meredith Oenning-Hodgson it is Parkinson's Disease. Her days and nights consist of dualistic power battles, of feelings of resignation, or of enduring the hours when her body freezes and she becomes a statue, at the mercy of Parkinson's Disease.

288 Pages
Paperback
978-1-63051-700-7 $22.95
Hardcover
978-1-63051-701-4 $32

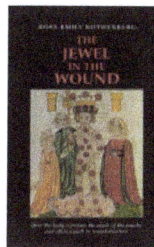

Rose-Emily Rothenberg

The Jewel in the Wound

How the Body Expresses the Needs of the Psyche and Offers a Path to Transformation

Rose-Emily Rothenberg explores wounding in a way that opens us to healing. It is the tale of a life lived consciously and with great integrity. She includes a rich variety of art work, images of cultural artifacts, and pictures from her visits with shamans.

216 Pages
Paperback
978-1-88860-216-6 $32
Hardcover
978-1-63051-035-0 $44.95

William Schoenl and Linda Schoenl

Jung's Evolving Views of Nazi Germany

From the Nazi Takeover to the End of World War II

This book describes for the first time Jung's views of Nazi Germany during the whole period from the Nazi takeover in 1933 to the end of World War II. It brings together the authors' research in archives and primary sources during the past 10 years.

99 Pages
Paperback
978-1-63051-407-5 $21.95
Hardcover
978-1-63051-408-2 $42

Lawrence H. Staples, PH.D.

Eighteen East 74th Street

An Autobiographical Novel

This book was written to share a lifelong struggle of the author to free himself from the powerfully dominating influence of his mother, something Jung more elegantly described as "The Battle for Deliverance from the Mother."

162 Pages
Paperback 978-1-63051-887-5 $21.95
Hardcover 978-1-63051-888-2 $32

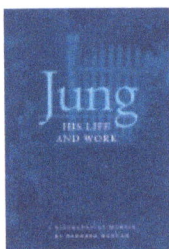

Barbara Hannah

Jung

His Life and Work

A Biographical Memoir

Published originally in 1976, this work has become a classic retelling of Jung's life and work by one of his most dedicated followers and intimate friends. Now back in print, this work deserves to occupy a place of importance in every Jungian library.

377 Pages
Paperback
978-1-88860-207-4 $28
Hardcover
978-1-63051-031-2 $65

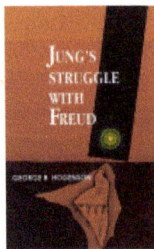

George B. Hogenson

Jung's Struggle with Freud

A Metabiological Study

An exploration of the historic relationship between Jung and Freud and its impact on twentieth-century thought.

192 Pages
Paperback
978-0-93302-981-1 $16.95
Hardcover
978-1-63051-014-5 $42

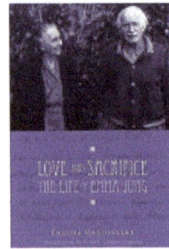

Imelda Gaudissart / Translated by Kathleen Llanwarne

Love and Sacrifice

The Life of Emma Jung

Little attention has been paid to Emma Jung's role in the history of analytical psychology and in the life of C.G. Jung. This extended biographical essay by Imelda Gaudissart, originally published in French, prov-ides a carefully detailed view of this remarkable woman.

216 Pages
Paperback
978-1-63051-085-5 $27
Hardcover
978-1-63051-086-2 $65

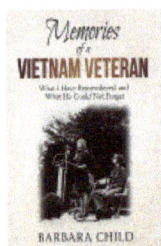

Barbara Child

Memories of a Vietnam Veteran

What I have Remembered and What He Could Not Forget

The book gives a partner's-eye view of post-traumatic stress and moral injury relentlessly taking their toll on the body, mind, and soul of a veteran who served as a medic in the Vietnam War. The book also shows how Jungian dream work with an expert, caring analyst can bring forth memories and the meaning of memories both sought and unsought.

194 Pages
Paperback
978-1-63051-691-8 $21.95
Hardcover
978-1-63051-692-5 $32

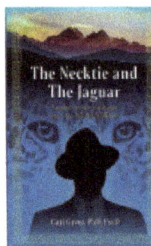

Carl Greer, PhD, PsyD

The Necktie and the Jaguar

A Memoir to Help You Change Your Story and Find Fulfillment

The Necktie and The Jaguar is a memoir with thought-provoking questions that encourage self-exploration. Author Carl Greer—businessman, philanthropist, and retired Jungian analyst and clinical psychologist—offers an illuminating roadmap to individuation and personal transformation.

304 Pages
Paperback
978-1-63051-903-2 $19.95
Hardcover
978-1-63051-904-9 $37

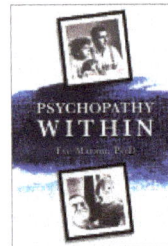

Eve Maram

Psychopathy Within

Psychopathy Within offers a new way of conceptualizing and defining psychopathy that is a convergence of the author's divergent professional experiences as a forensic psychologist and a Jungian-oriented psychotherapist and her personal life experiences over decades as a Jungian student and analysand.

292 Pages
Paperback
978-1-63051-375-7 $28
Hardcover
978-1-63051-376-4 $65

Judith Hubback

From Dawn to Dusk

Autobiography of Judith Hubback

Jungian analyst Judith Hubback is interested in studying change and the resistance to it in both patients and analysts, as well as enabling people to develop their full potential. She describes how she became a leading analyst in mid-life after working as a teacher, journalist, broadcaster and social researcher.

268 Pages
Paperback 978-1-63051-258-3 $21.95
Hardcover 978-1-63051-041-1 $27.95

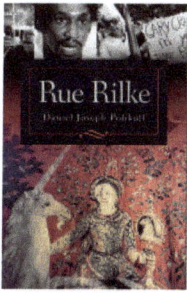

Daniel Joseph Polikoff

Rue Rilke

Travelogue, literary autobiography, and journalistic exposé of the mores of capital punishment, *Rue Rilke* chronicles its author's initiatory Rilke pilgrimage to France and Switzerland and—upon his return to America—his up-close involvement in death penalty.

288 Pages
Paperback 978-1-63051-358-0 $28
Hardcover 978-1-63051-359-7 $65

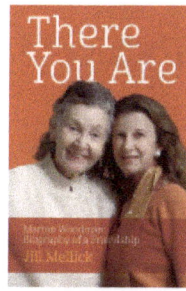

Jill Mellick

There You Are
Marion Woodman: Biography of a Friendship

How deep can a friendship go? Jill Mellick explores the grace, challenges, and gifts of an unexpected, instantly deep friendship with Marion Woodman. She documents with letters, calls, journals, memories, and photographs.

342 Pages
Paperback 978-1-63051-996-4 $34
Hardcover 978-1-63051-997-1 $49

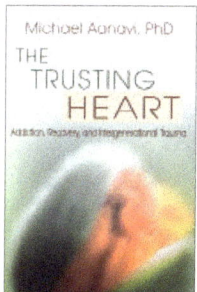

Michael Aanavi

The Trusting Heart
Addiction, Recovery, and Intergenerational Trauma

Dr. Michael Aanavi writes about his experience over the past twenty-plus years, both as a person in recovery and as a clinician. The book is about his exploration, his process and journey to inner growth and wholeness.

160 Pages
Available in Hardcover Only
978-1-63051-068-8 $26.95

Robert Brockway

Young Carl Jung

Young Carl Jung offers a balanced view with rare glimpses into Carl Jung's formative years. In a masterful telling of Jung's childhood, Brockway provides a clear perspective on the impact young Carl's experiences played in forming his later theories.

192 Pages
Paperback 978-1-88860-201-2 $26.95
Hardcover 978-1-63051-029-9 $37.95

Luis Moris
A Jungian Legacy
Tom Kirsch

This book honors the life and legacy of Tom Kirsch with essays from close friends of Tom who share how he touched their lives.

166 Pages
Paperback
978-1-63051-728-1 $23
Hardcover
978-1-63051-729-8 $32

Manisha Roy
My Four Homes
A Memoir

Manisha Roy recounts stories from her life, including visiting grandparents in the eastern part of Bengal through the process of becoming a Jungian analyst.

292 Pages
Paperback
978-1-63051-212-5 $21.95
Hardcover
978-1-63051-213-2 $42

Lawrence H. Staples, Ph.D.
Tearing Down Walls
Ich Bin Ein Berliner

Like Berlin, we all have a wall, an inner wall, that needs to be torn down. It's a wall we built at a young age, when socialization began and we needed a barrier behind which we could hide that part of ourselves that was unacceptable to our mothers as well as important others.

124 Pages
Paperback
978-1-68503-064-3 $21.95
Hardcover
978-1-68503-065-0 $34

CHIRON CLINICAL SERIES

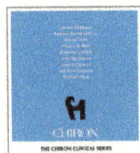

Murray Stein and Nathan Schwartz-Salant

Archetypal Processes in Psychotherapy

A collection of works on the study of Archetypal process by several Jungian analysts including Murray Stein, Thomas Kirsch, and Edward Whitmont.

235 Pages
Paperback 978-0-93302-912-5 $21.95
Hardcover 978-1-88860-274-6 $42

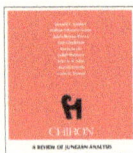

Nathan Schwartz-Salant, Murray Stein, and Various Authors

The Body in Analysis

Nathan Schwartz-Salant, Murray Stein, Joan Chodorow, Mario Jacoby, and several other Jungian analysts review the role of the body in psychoanalysis.

230 Pages
Paperback 978-0-93302-911-8 $27.95
Hardcover 978-1-88860-269-2 $44

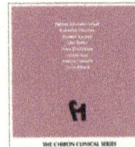

Murray Stein and Nathan Schwartz-Salant

The Borderline Personality in Analysis

This story details Jung's friendships with Mary Mellon and J. B. Priestley, who both admired him and helped make his psychology known and recognized throughout the world. In this book, we get a glimpse of Jung the man, with "nose and ears," as his son Franz said of him—a remarkable genius but also a man with ordinary human strivings and flaws.

288 Pages
Paperback 978-0-93302-913-2 $27.95
Hardcover 978-1-88860-278-4 $44

Various Authors

Dreams in Analysis

A collection of works on the study of dreams by several Jungian analysts including Murray Stein, Thomas Kirsch, and Edward Whitmont.

242 Pages
Paperback 978-0-93302-920-0 $21.95
Hardcover 978-1-88860-282-1 $42

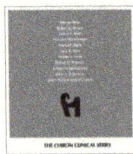

Nathan Salant-Schwartz and Murray Stein

Liminality and Transitional Phenomena

Nathan Schwartz-Salant, Murray Stein and several other Jungian analysts review Liminality and Transitional Phenomena in psychoanalysis.

204 Pages
Paperback 978-0-93302-929-3 $21.95
Hardcover 978-1-88860-287-6 $42

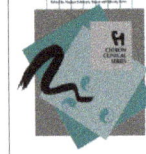

Nathan Schwartz-Salant

Gender & Soul in Psychotherapy

A collection of works on the study of gender and soul by several Jungian analysts including Murray Stein, Nathan Schwartz-Salant, and Edward Whitmont.

306 Pages
Paperback 978-0-93302-951-4 $21.95
Hardcover 978-1-88860-296-8 $42

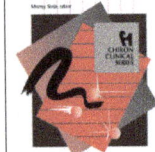

Murray Stein

The Interactive Field in Analysis, Volume 1

The interactive field in analysis may be thought of as an uninvited guest in the session. Presenting contemporary views on interpretation and the interactive field, these essays from leaders in the world of analytical psychology provide theory and examples of how to encounter and make use of this field.

160 Pages
Paperback 978-0-93302-977-4 $27.95
Hardcover 978-1-63051-022-0 $44

Murray Stein

Mad Parts of Sane People in Analysis

Clinical material on madness includes: *Sectarian and Titanic Madness* by Rafael Lopez-Pedraza, *Notes on the Counterpart* by Michael Eigen, and *General Gordon's Constant Object* by Alfred Plaut, among others.

240 Pages
Paperback 978-0-93302-967-5 $14.95
Hardcover 978-1-63051-010-7 $42

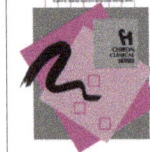

Murray Stein and Nathan Schwartz-Salant

Transference Countertransference

Fundamental issues of transference and countertransference are examined in such areas as sexual acting-out, dreams, eating disorders, successful and unsuccessful interventions, borderline disorders, and psychological types. Papers by Schwartz-Salant, Woodman, Stein, De Shong Meador, and Beebe, among others.

200 Pages
Paperback 978-1-63051-246-0 $27.95
Hardcover 978-1-88860-266-1 $44

CHIRON LEGACY
Released with Recollections, LLC

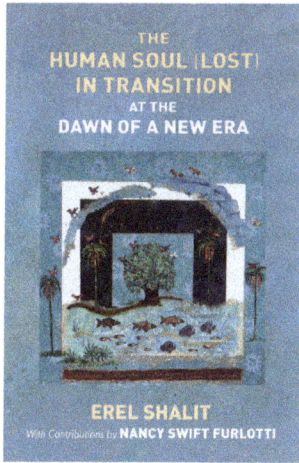

Erel Shalit

The Human Soul (Lost) in Transition At the Dawn of a New Era

"The aim of this book," wrote Shalit, "is to present a depth psychological perspective on phenomena pertaining to the present, postmodern era. As such, its origins are in the depths; symbolically, in the depth of the waters, in which the sacred is reflected."

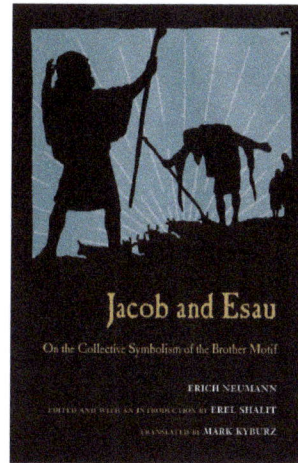

246 Pages
Paperback
978-1-63051-682-6 $29.00
Hardcover
978-1-63051-683-3 $47.00

Erich Neumann

Jacob & Esau
On the Collective Symbolism of the Brother Motif

Erich Neumann elaborates on the central role of the principle of opposites in the human soul, contrasting Jacob's introversion with Esau's extraversion, the sacred and the profane, the inner and the outer aspects of the God-image, the shadow and its projection, and how the old ethic—expressed, for example, in the expulsion of the scapegoat—perpetuates evil.

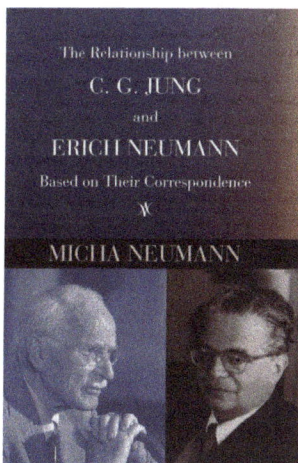

182 Pages
Paperback
978-1-63051-216-3 $21.95
Hardcover
978-1-63051-217-0 $32.00

Micha Neumann

The Relationship between C.G. Jung and Erich Neumann
Based on Their Correspondence

Based on the letters of Jung and Neumann, which have been recently published, along with the impressions Micha Neumann gleaned from his parents, this book provides a framework for this correspondence and provides additional insight into a rich, personal dimension of their complicated relationship.

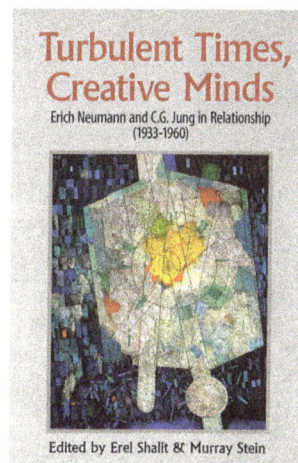

84 Pages
Paperback
978-1-63051-219-4 $21.95
Hardcover
978-1-63051-220-0 $32.00

Erel Shalit & Murray Stein

Turbulent Times, Creative Minds
Erich Neumann and C.G. Jung in Relationship (1934-1960)

This volume of essays by well-known Jungian analysts and scholars provides the most comprehensive comparison to date between the works of C.G. Jung and Erich Neumann.

468 Pages
Paperback
978-1-63051-445-7 $34
Hardcover
978-1-63051-363-4 $75

COMPLEXES & ARCHETYPES

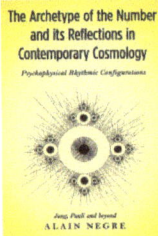

Alain Negre

The Archetype of the Number and its Reflections in Contemporary Cosmology

Through the reflection of the archetypal number, detected as "rhythmic configurations of energy" in the history of the universe, author Alain Negre reveals un-precedented links between certain events in this story and raises the questions of their use in theoretical physics as an aid in interpreting and in suggesting new avenues of research.

212 Pages
Paperback 978-1-63051-438-9 $26
Hardcover 978-1-63051-439-6 $39

Violet Sherwood, PHD

Haunted

The Death Mother Archetype

The disturbing experience of psychological infanticide reflects the darkest aspect of the wounding of the Sacred Feminine – the Death Mother archetype that annihilates rather than nurtures life.

314 Pages
Paperback 978-1-63051-988-9 $29
Hardcover 978-1-63051-989-6 $42

Lynne Radomsky

Where Dreams Come Alive

The Alchemy of the African Healer

This work explores the deep archetypal patterns embedded in the African healing initiation, the alchemical opus, and the individuation process through the work of C.G. Jung.

224 Pages
Paperback
978-1-63051-708-3 $32
Hardcover
978-1-63051-709-0 $49

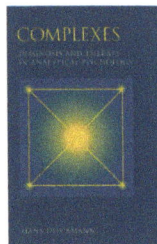

Hans Dieckmann

Complexes

Diagnosis and Therapy in Analytical Psychology

Complexes provides a clear and orderly path through the chaotic contents of analysis.

140 Pages
Paperback
978-1-88860-209-8 $21.95
Hardcover
978-1-63051-032-9 $50

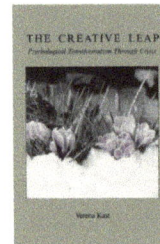

Verena Kast

The Creative Leap

Psychological Transformation through Crisis

The practical execution of crisis intervention in psychotherapeutic practice and Jungian Analysis.

136 Pages
Paperback
978-0-93302-932-3 $21.95
Hardcover
978-1-88860-286-9 $32

CREATIVITY

Harry A. Wilmer

Creativity

Paradoxes & Reflections

Essays on the paradoxes and reflections of creativity: autobiography, literary biography, music, science, drama, poetry, storytelling, criticism, parageography, and war.

210 Pages
Paperback 978-0-93302-944-6 $14.95
Hardcover 978-1-88860-294-4 $42

Susan M. Tiberghien

Écrire Vers la Plénitude: Leçons inspirées par C.G. Jung

S'appuyant sur les écrits de C.G. Jung et d'autres grands auteurs–Maître Eckhart, Rainer Maria Rilke, Etty Hillesum, Thomas Merton—Susan M. Tiberghien réunit la psychologie, la spiritualité et les arts, et offre ainsi à ses lecteurs un chemin vers la plénitude.

236 Pages
Paperback 978-1-63051-891-2 $16.95
Hardcover 978-1-63051-892-9 $32

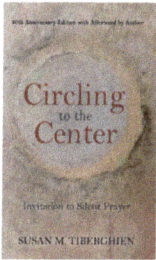

Susan M. Toberghien

Circling to the Center
Invitation to Silent Prayer

In this 20th Anniversary Edition, Tiberghien writes an Afterword to update her journey, opening the confines of her own darkness and finding atonement in the natural world and in the presence of Sophia, the "hidden wholeness" of creation.

166 Pages
Paperback 978-1-63051-740-3 $18.95
Hardcover 978-1-63051-741-0 $32

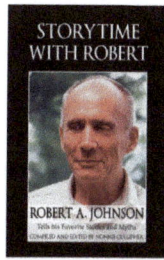

Robert A. Johnson

Storytime with Robert
Robert A. Johnson Tells His Favorite Stories and Myths

Robert A. Johnson was more than an international best-selling author of fifteen books, brilliant and influential Jungian analyst, and acclaimed international lecturer; he was a master storyteller. This collection is transcribed from Robert's own tellings throughout the years. Robert told these stories, his favorites, to an appreciative and revering community each night at Journey into Wholeness events from 1981 to 2001.

122 Pages
Paperback 978-1-63051-862-2 $16.95
Hardcover 978-1-63051-863-9 $27.95

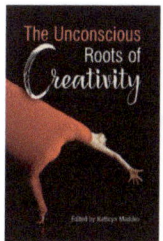

Kathryn Madden

The Unconscious Roots of Creativity

From whence spring the sparks of creativity? It is to this very question that the field of depth psychology—especially that of C.G. Jung and his intellectual descendants—has much to contribute.

350 Pages
Paperback
978-1-63051-385-6 $34
Hardcover
978-1-63051-386-3 $65

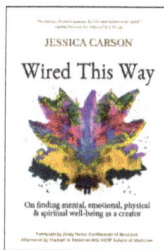

Jessica Carson

Wired This Way
On Finding Mental, Emotional, Physical, and Spiritual Well-Being as a Creator

Wired This Way explores why mental health issues, burnout, and stress-related illness among entrepreneurs are not due to weakness, but to a rich inner complexity that's prone to imbalance. Using tools of self-study, entrepreneurs can harness all that they are—their light and dark—to create with health and fulfillment.

226 Pages
Paperback 978-1-63051-796-0 $21.95
Hardcover 978-1-63051-797-7 $32

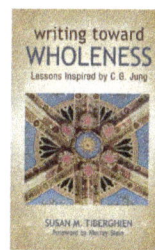

Susan M. Tiberghien

Writing Towards Wholeness
Lessons Inspired by C.G. Jung

In focusing on insights and excerpts from C.G. Jung's writings, and from many other inspirational writers, Susan M. Tiberghien brings together psychology, spirituality, and the arts, offering a way to wholeness. From its first pages, *Writing Toward Wholeness* encourages readers to embark on their own journey through writing toward selfhood, toward wholeness. At every step, it reinforces the lessons C.G. Jung learned and shared with millions of people.

234 Pages
Paperback 978-1-63051-454-9 $18.95
Hardcover 978-1-63051-455-6 $34

DREAMS & ACTIVE IMAGINATION

Rose-Emily Rothenberg

An Orphan's Odyssey
Sacred Journeys to Renewal

In *An Orphan's Odyssey*, Rose-Emily Rothenberg explores the images and symbols that appeared in the stories, myths, and dreams surrounding her travels to Africa, reconnecting her to ancestors, both human and animal, who helped her access her cultural roots.

232 Pages
Paperback 978-1-63051-195-1 $19.95
Hardcover 978-1-63051-196-8 $42

Sheila Dickman Zarrow

Friendship and Healing
The Dreams of John Adams and Benjamin Rush

The letters of John Adams and Benjamin Rush depict the friendship that grew between the two as the course of history brought change into their lives and forced them to change themselves. Of particular interest are the dreams both Founding Fathers described in their letters and the evidence Sheila Zarrow has uncovered about how they considered the effects of their dreams.

140 Pages
Paperback 978-1-88860-250-0 $14.95
Hardcover 978-1-63051-059-6 $37.95

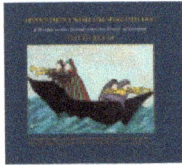

David Blum

Appointment with the Wise Old Dog
A Bridge to the Transformative Power of Dreams

This book provides the necessary, comprehensive complement to David Blum's highly regarded 1998 documentary that crystallized his inner work as it related to his cancer experience.

123 Pages
Paperback 978-1-63051-924-7 $39
Hardcover 978-1-63051-870-7 $47

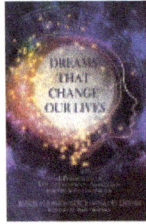

Robert J. Hoss & Robert P. Gongloff

Dreams that Change Our Lives
A Publication of The International Association for the Study of Dreams

Suppose you could take action in your dream to eliminate a recurring nightmare, heal a relationship, or even a physical ailment. The 100 dreamers in this book have!

362 Pages
Paperback 978-1-63051-429-7 $29.95
Hardcover 978-1-63051-430-3 $49

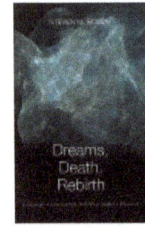

Steven M. Rosen

Dreams, Death, Rebirth
A Topological Odyssey into Alchemy's Hidden Dimensions

Steven M. Rosen explores the profound mystery of death and rebirth from psychological, philosophical, and alchemical perspectives.

268 Pages
Paperback 978-1-63051-279-8 $28
Hardcover 978-1-63051-084-8 $65

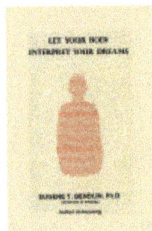

Eugene T. Gendlin

Let Your Body Interpret Your Dreams

This helpful *how* to book derives questions from many existing theories to aid the dreamer in the process of interpretation. It teaches the reader to recognize certain bodily responses that may hold the key to a breakthrough.

200 Pages
Paperback 978-0-93302-901-9 $21.95
Hardcover 978-1-88860-271-5 $42

James Hollis

Hauntings
Dispelling the Ghosts Who Run Our Lives

James Hollis considers one's transformation through the invisible world—how we are all governed by the presence of invisible forms—spirits, ghosts, ancestral and parental influences, inner voices, dreams, impulses, untold stories, complexes, synchronicities, and mysteries—which move through us, and through history.

176 Pages
Paperback 978-1-63051-349-8 $21.95
Hardcover 978-1-63051-368-9 $42

Phyllis Stowell

Transformations
Nearing the End of Life: Dreams and Visions

Transformations, by Phyllis Stowell, is a story of five years of analysis told from the point of view of the woman dreaming.

180 Pages
Paperback
978-1-63051-724-3 $21.95
Hardcover
978-1-63051-725-0 $29

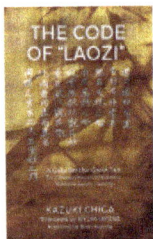

Kazuki Chiga

The Code of Laozi
A Gate for the Great Tao— The Ultimate Principle of Sexuality Hidden in Laozi's Teaching

This book is a translation of "The Code of Laozi" ("Tao Code" translated literally), written by Kazuki Chiga, originally published in Japanese in 2009. He visited an unexplored region associated with a wise man in China, Laozi, had unexpected experiences, and learned the Tao of Laozi.

150 Pages
Paperback 978-1-63051-916-2 $26.95
Hardcover 978-1-63051-917-9 $34

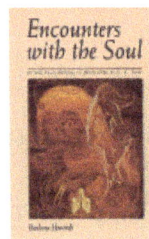

Barbara Hannah

Encounters with the Soul
Active Imagination as Developed by C.G. Jung

Barbara Hannah, Jungian analyst and author, explores Jung's method of "active imagination," often considered the most powerful tool in analytical psychology for achieving direct contact with the unconscious and attaining greater inner awareness. Using historical and contemporary case studies, Hannah traces the human journey toward personal wholeness.

264 Pages
Paperback 978-1-63051-350-4 $28
Hardcover 978-1-63051-034-3 $65

FAIRYTALES

Collected Works of Marie-Louise von Franz Volume 1
Archetypal Symbols in Fairytales: The Profane and Magical Worlds

Fairytales, like myths, provide a cultural and societal backdrop that helps the human imagination narrate the meaning of life's events. The remarkable similarities in fairytale motifs across different lands and cultures inspired many scholars to search for the original homeland of fairytales. While peregrinations of fairytale motifs occur, the common root of fairytales is more archetypal than geographic.

608 Pages
Paperback 978-1-63051-854-7 $42
Hardcover 978-1-63051-855-4 $69

Collected Works of Marie-Louise von Franz Volume 2
Archetypal Symbols in Fairytales: The Hero's Journey

The *Hero's Journey* is about the great adventure that leads to a cherished and difficult to obtain prize. In these fairytales, the Self is often symbolized as that treasured prize and the hero's travails symbolize the process of individuation.

476 Pages
Paperback 978-1-63051-950-6 $42
Hardcover 978-1-63051-951-3 $69

Collected Works of Marie-Louise von Franz Volume 3
Archetypal Symbols in Fairytales: The Maiden's Quest

The maiden/heroine navigates a complicated maze of inner and outer relationships as she builds a bridge to the unconscious. The heroine contends with the *animus* in many forms like a devouring and incestuous father, demonic groom, the beautiful prince, an androgenous mother, a cold dark tower, and through conflict with the evil stepmother.

520 Pages
Paperback 978-1-63051-960-5 $42
Hardcover 978-1-63051-961-2 $69

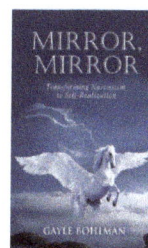

Gayle Bohlman

Mirror, Mirror
Transforming Narcissism to Self-Realization

This book offers an in-depth exploration of narcissism, looking at how it is constructed and a transformative path of healing narcissistic wounds utilizing the mirrors in the stories of Snow White, Narcissus, and Medusa to explicate a path from narcissism to self-realization.

140 Pages
Paperback 978-1-63051-704-5 $16.95
Hardcover 978-1-63051-705-2 $27

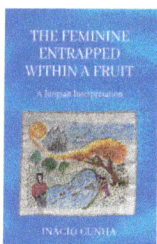

Inácio Cunha

The Feminine Entrapped Within a Fruit
A Jungian Interpretation

The main purpose of this book is to investigate the archetypal motif of the feminine entrapped within vegetable species (mainly fruits). Several fairy tales originating in different regions (America, Europe, Africa and Eastern countries) were analyzed. Each one of these tales illustrates how the unconscious symbolizes the ordeals the feminine principle has gone through (and still goes through!) in the collective consciousness, as well as how the unconscious may deal with it.

139 Pages
Paperback 978-1-68503-017-9 $19.95
Hardcover 978-1-68503-018-6 $29

Hallfridur J. Ragnheidardottir

Quest for the Mead of Poetry
Menstrual Symbolism in Icelandic Folk and Fairy Tales

A translation and interpretation of seven Icelandic tales. In search for the meaning of a dream in which she was given a silver necklace by a poet, the author happened upon the key to hidden layers of her ancestral heritage. It was a revelation that led her to understand that the tabooed menstrual flow of her ancestresses found expression in symbolic language.

246 Pages
Paperback 978-1-63051-369-6 $28
Hardcover 978-1-63051-370-2 $65

Murray Stein and Lionel Corbett

Psyche's Stories *Volume 1*

Modern Jungian Interpretations of Fairy Tales

Fairy tales can reveal a hidden side of our lives, our unconscious, and our inter-relationship with others. Each of these essays provides a Jungian interpretation of a well-known or rare fairy tale to reveal the universal psychic dynamics that affect us in our lives and collectively in the world around us. In this volume, *Allerleirauh, Beauty and the Beast, The Wonderful Sheep, Cinderella, Cupid and Psyche, The Devil's Sooty Brother, The Fisherman and His Wife, Fitcher's Bird* and *The Goose Girl* are examined.

184 Pages
Paperback 978-1-63051-265-1 $27.95
Hardcover 978-1-88860-298-2 $65

*Murray Stein and Lionel Corbett
Essays by Claire Douglas, Lee Roloff, Tom Kapacinskas and others*

Psyche's Stories Volume 2

Modern Jungian Interpretations of Fairy Tales

In this volume, *Maid Maleen, The Old Woman in the Wood, Oisin's Mother, Rapunzel, The Snow Queen, Sunahsepa and Akanandun, The Water of Life, The White Snake, Snow White, Cinderella and Dracula* are examined.

192 Pages
Paperback 978-0-93302-956-9 $26.95
Hardcover 978-1-63051-006-0 $65

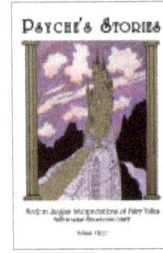

Murray Stein and Lionel Corbett

Psyche's Stories

Volume 3

Modern Jungian Interpretations of Fairy Tales

In this volume, *The White Snake, Clever Elsie, The Girl Without Hands, Snow White, Cinderella, Pinocchio, The Tsar, His Son*, and the *Swan Princess* are examined.

136 Pages
Paperback
978-0-93302-990-3 $26.95
Hardcover
978-1-63051-017-6 $37.95

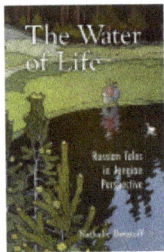

Nathalie Baratoff

The Water of Life
Russian Tales in Jungian Perspective

C.G. Jung's psychology provides a unique understanding of the seven tales in this volume. The archetypal images therein are many-layered. We can see them from the mythological viewpoint as dragons, demons and witches; we find them in rivers of fire, in kingdoms at the bottom of the sea, in talking animals, and in endless transformations that defy human experience.

326 Pages
Paperback 978-1-63051-879-0 $29
Hardcover 978-1-63051-880-6 $42

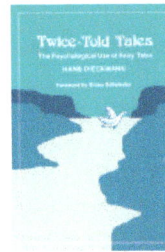

Hans Dieckmann

Twice-Told Tales
The Psychological Use of Fairy Tales

By the use of case histories, Hans Dieckmann recounts ways in which "the greatest treasures of the soul" can be revealed in fairy tales. He interprets the symbolic significance of many individual fairy tales and relates their meaning to various stages of a person's development.

154 Pages
Available in Paperback Only
978-0-93302-902-6 $21.95

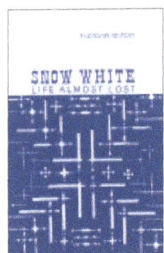

Theodor Seifert

Snow White
Life Almost Lost

The central problem Theodor Seifert treats in his interpretation of "Snow White" is relationship: "Can my frozen feelings come to life again?" "Can I make a new beginning, or must I live out a living death?"

142 Pages
Paperback 978-0-93302-908-8 $18.95
Hardcover 978-1-88860-273-9 $26.95

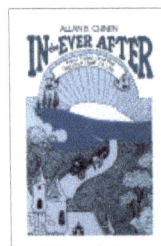

Allan B. Chinen

In the Ever After
Fairy Tales and the Second Half of Life

These rare fairy tales reveal a deep folk wisdom about the psychological tasks encountered in the second half of life. Collected from around the world, these stories offer an engaging exploration into the problems of adulthood and aging.

216 Pages
Available in Paperback Only
978-0-93302-941-5 $26.95

FICTION

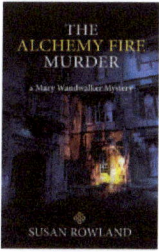

Susan Rowland
The Alchemy Fire Murder
A Mary Wandwalker Mystery

Former Archivist Mary Wandwalker hates bringing bad news. Nevertheless, she confirms to her alma mater that their prized medieval alchemy scroll, is, in fact, a seventeenth century copy. Given that the authentic artefact is needed for her Oxford college to survive, retrieving it is essential.

352 Pages
Paperback 978-1-68503-129-9 $19.95
Hardcover 978-1-68503-130-5 $37

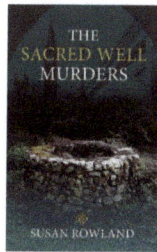

Susan Rowland
The Sacred Well Murders

A simple job turns deadly when Mary Wandwalker, novice detective, is hired to chaperone a young American, Rhiannon, to the Oxford University Summer School on the ancient Celts.

336 Pages
Paperback
978-1-68503-005-6 $16.95
Hardcover
978-1-68503-006-3 $32

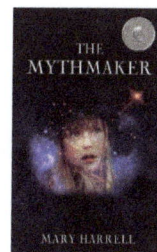

Mary Harrell
The Mythmaker

A personal myth, a fiction, based on author and depth psychologist Dr. Mary Harrell's life. After the sudden death of her mother, seven young children and an overwhelmed father were left to figure out what to do.

148 Pages
Paperback
978-1-63051-500-3 $16.95
Hardcover
978-1-63051-501-0 $27

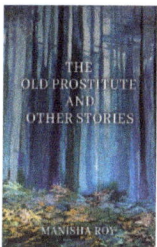

Manisha Roy
The Old Prostitute and Other Stories

Manisha Roy shares her love of writing in this collection of over 20 short stories. The stories of this collection were written over a span of several decades beginning in 1985 and ending in 2022.

214 Pages
Paperback 978-1-68503-091-9 $16.95
Hardcover 978-1-68503-092-6 $32

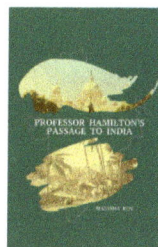

Manisha Roy
Professor Hamilton's Passage to India

In 1975, Dr. Charles Hamilton, Professor of Infectious Diseases from a respected medical school in the U.S. visited India after receiving a substantial research grant.

286 Pages
Paperback 978-1-68503-013-1 $19.95
Hardcover 978-1-68503-014-8 $32

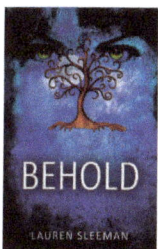

Lauren Sleeman
Behold

Jung's symbols and archetypes inspired the mystical world of this book. Alchemy also plays a significant role in this magical fantasy, a journey of personal and collective transformation. The many layers of archetypal consciousness in human experience are brought to light in a humorous yet "instructive" way.

216 Pages
Paperback 978-1-63051-972-8 $19.95
Hardcover 978-1-63051-973-5 $32

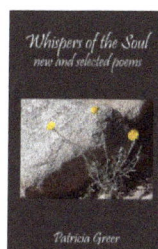

Patricia Greer
Whispers of the Soul
New and Selected Poems

A collection of poems that range from expressions of gratitude for the gifts of nature, to musings about aging and the fragility of life, to insights about women's issues and concerns, to observations about the complexities of family dynamics, to reflections about writing and therapy.

144 Pages
Paperback 978-1-63051-995-7 $16.95
Hardcover 978-1-63051-993-3 $29

Marie Newton
Dizzy and the Dreams

What surprises await us with our first encounter with the unconscious, coincidence, and mysterious ways of knowing? Dizzy's portal into these realms that were explored by the great Swiss psychologist C. G. Jung is an engaging and ultimately joyful tale of such first encounters.

66 Pages
Paperback
978-1-63051-768-7 $8.95
Hardcover
978-1-63051-769-4 $19.95

David E. Peeler
Lost and Found in East Jesus

Appalachian folklore, echoes of a Biblical apocalypse, life in a circus town and more come together in the debut short story collection by David E. Peeler.

158 Pages
Paperback
978-1-63051-908-7 $16.95
Hardcover
978-1-63051-909-4 $29

Roula-Marie Dib
Simply Being

A celebration of the various facets of life, its blessings, beauties, and challenges.

82 Pages
Paperback
978-1-63051-925-4 $14.95
Hardcover
978-1-63051-926-1 $22.95

GENDER STUDIES

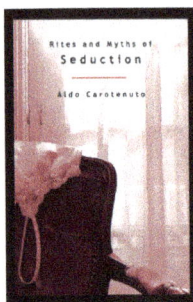

Aldo Carotenuto
Rites and Myths of Seduction

This book fosters a clear understanding of the affective roots of seduction that can lead to transformation and the discovery of a new identity.

226 Pages
Available in Paperback Only
978-1-88860-219-7 $21.95

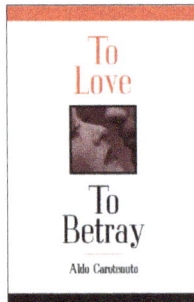

Aldo Carotenuto
To Love To Betray

Jungian analyst Aldo Carotenuto shows us the positive and fundamental role of betrayal in our growth throughout life. Carotenuto applies the term to betray to many issues brought to psychotherapy.

202 Pages
Available in Paperback Only
978-1-63051-249-1 $26.95

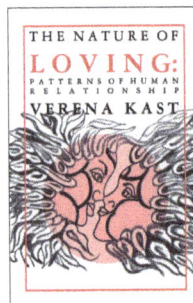

Verena Kast
Nature of Loving
Patterns of Human Relationship

Focusing primarily on the relationship between the sexes, this work also includes much that is relevant to other forms of human intimacy. Myth is brought alive and illuminates the present with the intense light cast by archetypal understandings.

114 Pages
Paperback 978-0-93302-906-4 $21.95
Hardcover 978-1-88860-272-2 $42

Ann Ulanov and Barry Ulanov
The Witch and the Clown
Two Archetypes of Human Sexuality

The Ulanovs examine the images of the witch and the clown, representing psychic factors, which are revealed as determining much of the complexity of human sexual life. The common notions of male sexuality based upon strength and aggression and female sexuality upon weakness and submission are thoroughly undone in this analysis.

350 Pages
Paperback 978-0-93302-907-1 $27.95
Hardcover 978-1-63051-028-2 $44

Helmut Barz

For Men, Too

A Grateful Critique of Feminism

The strongest impulse leading Helmut Barz to write this book was his conviction that the women's movement is, or should be, just as much a matter for men as for women. He responds as one male human, to the discovery—described for the most part by women—that the history of humanity over the past several thousand years has also been a history of the oppression of women by men.

146 Pages
Available in Paperback Only
978-0-93302-942-2 $21.95

Peter Schellenbaum

How to Say No to the One You Love

Maintaining one's identity while becoming involved in the emotional life of another has become a particular challenge for modern couples. Peter Schellenbaum explores the problem of boundaries within intimacy in both successful and unsuccessful relationships.

144 Pages
Available in Hardcover Only
978-0-93302-925-5 $42

Mary E. Loomis

Her Father's Daughter

When Women Succeed in a Man's World

Mary Loomis uncovers the inner price of living up to masculine expectations and definitions of success. She shows women how to break those ties, move through their hidden shame, and take charge of their own destinies.

120 Pages
Paperback 978-0-93302-988-0 $14.95
Hardcover 978-1-63051-021-3 $42

Harry A. Wilmer

Mother Father

This collection of autobiographical and biographical essays examines the many roles of mother and father, both personal and cultural, in the psychological life and development of the individual.

204 Pages
Paperback 978-1-63051-259-0 $21.95
Hardcover 978-1-88860-290-6 $42

GRIEF & LOSS

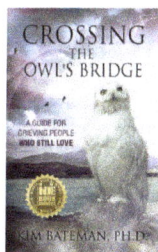

Kim Bateman

Crossing the Owl's Bridge

A Guide for Grieving People Who Still Love

Crossing the Owl's Bridge uses the wisdom of worldwide folk tales to demonstrate how to share, ritualize, and transform grief. The premise is that although we do have to say goodbye to our material relationship, we are also being presented with a chance to say hello to a different type of relationship. *Crossing the Owl's Bridge* illustrates creative outcomes to mourning that allow one to recognize, contain, release, and yet stay in relationship and keep loving.

184 Pages
Paperback 978-1-63051-372-6 $16.95
Hardcover 978-1-63051-373-3 $42

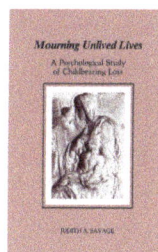

Judith Savage

Mourning Unlived Lives

A Psychological Study of Childbearing Loss

Of course this book will be used as a survival manual for grieving parents, but it is a remarkable kit for the biggest psychological project of our time: ordinary people teaching themselves to work through even the saddest occasions in order to live with strong feeling.

142 Pages
Paperback 978-0-93302-940-8 $21.95
Hardcover 978-1-88860-283-8 $42

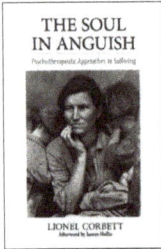

Lionel Corbett

The Soul in Anguish

Psychotherapeutic Approaches to Suffering

The Soul in Anguish presents a variety of approaches to psychotherapeutic work with suffering people, from the perspectives of both Jungian and psychoanalytic psychology. An important theme of the book is the impact of suffering—suffering may be harmful or helpful to the development of the personality.

380 Pages
Paperback 978-1-63051-235-4 $28
Hardcover 978-1-63051-236-1 $65

Charlotte Mathes

And a Sword Shall Pierce Your Heart

Moving from Despair to Meaning after the Death of a Child

Jungian psychoanalyst Charlotte Mathes experienced a parent's worst nightmare—the death of her child. In this book, she describes her experience of struggling to find meaning and wholeness in one of the most shattering of experiences.

314 Pages
Paperback 978-1-88860-234-0 $16.95
Hardcover 978-1-63051-047-3 $42

INDIVIDUATION AND THE STAGES OF LIFE

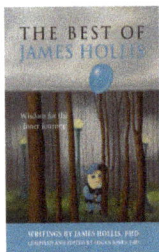

James Hollis, PHD

The Best of James Hollis

Wisdom for the Inner Journey

A collection of excerpts from the writings of James Hollis, these selections, compiled by editor Logan Jones, span across his body of work from *The Middle Passage* (1993) to *Prisms* (2021) organized into different topics ranging from the psychological concepts of Carl Jung to the everyday tasks of our living and callings.

336 Pages
Paperback 978-1-63051-976-6 $26.95
Hardcover 978-1-63051-977-3 $42

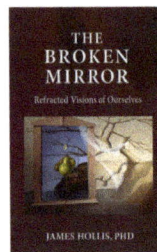

James Hollis, PHD

The Broken Mirror

Refracted Visions of Ourselves

This book explores the need to know ourselves more deeply, and the many obstacles that stand in our way. The various chapters illustrate internal obstacles such as intimidation by the magnitude of the project, the readiness to avoid the hard work, and gnawing self-doubt, but also provide tools to strengthen consciousness to take these obstacles on.

216 Pages
Paperback 978-1-68503-009-4 $24.95
Hardcover 978-1-68503-010-0 $40

James Hollis, PHD

Prisms

Reflections on This Journey We Call Life

James Hollis explores the roadblocks we encounter and our on-going challenge to live our brief journey with as much courage, insight, and resolve as we can bring to the table.

220 Pages
Paperback 978-1-63051-929-2 $26.95
Hardcover 978-1-63051-930-8 $40

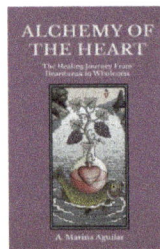

A. Marina Aguilar

Alchemy of the Heart

The Healing Journey From Heartbreak to Wholeness

Heartbreak can lead to depression and even despair or, alternatively, act as a profound initiation onto the path of Individuation. The author discovers a healing myth for not only herself, but for a heartbroken world in the love story of Dionysos and Ariadne.

210 Pages
Paperback 978-1-63051-450-1 $24.95
Hardcover 978-1-63051-451-8 $47

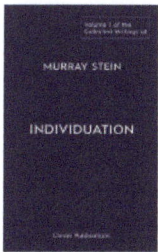

Murray Stein

Collected Writings of Murray Stein Volume 1

Individuation

Volume 1 contains a core element of Dr. Stein's lifelong teaching, namely the concept of individuation. The process of individuation fosters the fulfillment of unconscious potential as called forth by the archetypal Self.

348 Pages
Paperback 978-1-63051-760-1 $37
Hardcover 978-1-63051-761-8 $75

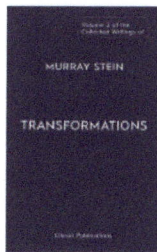

Murray Stein

Collected Writings of Murray Stein Volume 3

Transformations

Transformation suggests a profound change in life, often of a psychological or spiritual nature. In Volume 3, Dr. Stein examines this developmental process on a personal as well as a cultural level.

316 Pages
Paperback 978-1-63051-941-4 $39
Hardcover 978-1-63051-942-1 $75

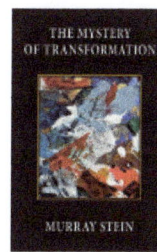

Murray Stein

The Mystery of Transformation

This work consists of a series of probes into the mystery of the individuation process. Central to the discussion are Jung's late writings on the alchemy of psychological transformation in the late stages of individuation.

248 Pages
Paperback 978-1-68503-068-1 $29
Hardcover 978-1-68503-069-8 $42

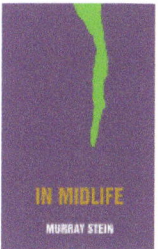

Murray Stein

In Midlife

A Jungian Perspective

Midlife: crisis, anger, change… Drawing on analytic experience, dreams, and myths, Murray Stein, a well-known analyst, formulates the three main features of the middle passage.

158 Pages
Paperback 978-1-63051-089-3 $24.95
Hardcover 978-1-63051-090-9 $65

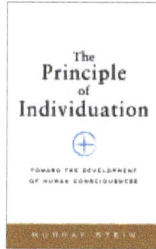

Murray Stein

The Principle of Individuation

Toward the Development of Human Consciousness

The Principle of Individuation suggests new approaches, on both personal and communal levels, for gaining freedom from the compulsion to repeat endlessly the dysfunctional patterns that have conditioned us. In this concise and contemporary account of the process of individuation, Murray Stein sets out its two basic movements and then examines the central role of numinous experience, the critical importance of initiation, and the unique psychic space required for its unfolding.

240 Pages
Paperback 978-163051-264-4 $28
Hardcover 978-1-63051-053-4 $65

Joan Chamberlain Engelsman

The Queen's Cloak
A Myth for Mid-Life

This original fairy tale about a queen who weaves herself a magic cloak draws the reader in through the use of traditional fairy-tale surroundings and provides a pointed metaphor for the struggles many women encounter in mid-life. A discussion which helps to establish a model for self-healing follows.

128 Pages
Available in Paperback Only
978-1-63051-257-6 $21.95

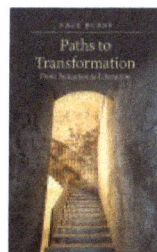

Kate Burns

Paths to Transformation
From Initiation to Liberation

It is our nature to transform ourselves from time to time; to cling to old ways is to resist a fundamental law of nature-death before rebirth. In *Paths to Transformation*, Kate Burns traces this process, correlating it with rituals of initiation and amplifying the stages with a rich collection of images, dreams, and case studies.

128 Pages
Paperback 978-1-63051-286-6 $16.95
Hardcover 978-1-63051-078-7 $42

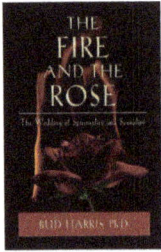

Bud Harris

The Fire and the Rose

The Wedding of Spirituality and Sexuality

Analyst Bud Harris, Ph.D., challenges us to reconsider our views of spirituality and sexuality as opposites and bring them into harmony and creativity. He encourages that together we can heal one of our culture's great wounds of the soul.

224 Pages
Paperback 978-1-63051-248-4 $26.95
Hardcover 978-1-63051-055-8 $37.95

Leslie Swain, Lionel Corbett, Michael Carbine

Jung and Aging

Possibilities and Potentials for the Second Half of Life

We need to better understand how to navigate the second half of life in ways that are productive and satisfying, and Jungian psychology, with its focus on the discovery of meaning and continuous development of the personality is especially helpful for addressing the concerns of aging.

271 Pages
Paperback 978-1-63051-968-1 $29
Hardcover 978-1-63051-969-8 $42

INNERQUEST BOOKS

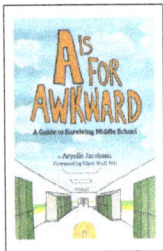

Aryelle Jacobsen

A is for Awkward

A Guide to Surviving Middle School

A guide for middle schoolers that alphabetizes the complications of adolescence and how to deal with them. Each page features a concept—like "E is for Encouragement" or "O is for Optimism"—advice related to the topic and original art by local teens. She hopes the book will encourage younger students and help them develop an attitude of optimism and gratitude.

36 Pages
Paperback 978-1-63051-442-6 $8.95
Hardcover 978-1-63051-443-3 $21.95

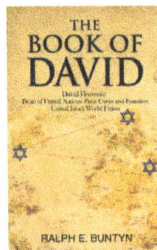

Ralph Buntyn

The Book of David

David Horowitz: Dean of United Nations Press Corps and Founder: United Israel World Union

For 10 years, author Ralph Buntyn spent many hours with renowned United Nations correspondent and United Israel founder David Horowitz. This book is based on his personal notes, extensive archival records and reflections from these conversations.

330 Pages
Paperback 978-1-63051-583-6 $18.95
Hardcover 978-1-63051-584-3 $32

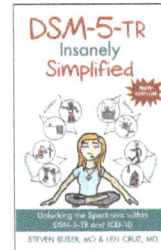

Steve Buser & Leonard Cruz

DSM-5-TR Insanely Simplified

Unlocking the Spectrums within DSM-5-TR and ICD-10

This book provides a summary of key concepts of the new diagnostic schema introduced in DSM-5 as well as the updated DSM-5-TR. It utilizes a variety of techniques to help clinicians master the new spectrum approach to diagnosis and its complex criteria.

152 Pages
Paperback 978-1-68503-044-5 $24.95
Hardcover 978-1-68503-045-2 $34.95

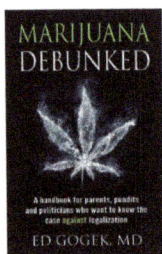

Ed Gogek

Marijuana Debunked

A Handbook for Parents, Pundits and Politicians Who Want to Know the Case Aagainst Legalization

This book presents the case against marijuana on an equal footing.

332 Pages
Paperback 978-1-63051-229-3 $16.95
Hardcover 978-1-63051-230-9 $26.95

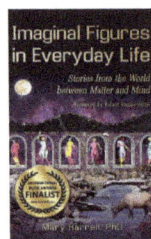

Mary Harrell

Imaginal Figures in Everyday Life

Stories from the World between Matter and Mind

Mary Harrell unflinchingly greets a cast of imaginal figures who inhabit her life, and encourages all of us to welcome their wisdom into our own inner landscapes.

178 Pages
Paperback 978-1-63051-354-2 $18.95
Hardcover 978-1-63051-355-9 $42

JUNG IN THE WORLD

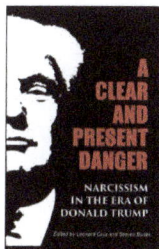

Leonard Cruz and Steven Buser

Narcissism in the Era of President Trump

President Trump's supporters as well as his detractors may be left asking how narcissistic traits manifest in someone who becomes president. This book assembles thoughtful, deep explorations of narcissism by bestselling authors, university professors, and practicing clinicians.

288 Pages
Paperback 978-1-63051-414-3 $18.95
Hardcover 978-1-63051-415-0 $47

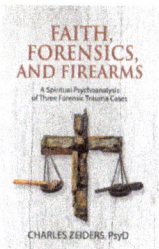

Charles Zeiders, PSYD

Faith, Forensics, and Firearms

A Spiritual Psychoanalysis of Three Forensic Trauma Cases

When one seeks civil redress for trauma, even a favorable outcome will not likely heal the heart of a plaintiff who has been raped, beaten, humiliated, violated, or treated unjustly. Forensic psychology analyzes human behavior as it applies to the law. The forensic psychologist establishes the merits of a case, then writes a report.

118 Pages
Paperback 978-1-63051-664-2 $21.95
Hardcover 978-1-63051-665-9 $27

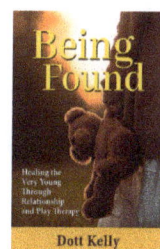

Dott Kelly

Being Found

Healing the Very Young Through Relationship & Play Therapy

The goal of the therapist is to find the child. When we have found the child, the child has also made an attempt at being seen. So there we are, face to face with the obstacles and disturbances between us.

310 Pages
Paperback
978-1-68503-107-7 $29
Hardcover
978-1-68503-109-1 $42

Lio Dajun / Zhang Wenzhi

The Book of Changes

An Introduction to the Zhou yi

The I Ching (a. k. a. Yi jing, the Book of Changes, Zhou Changes) is one of the oldest texts in world history, and it is often considered the "first in the Confucian classics." To help readers fully appreciate this archaic classical work, the author of this book comprehensively considers the explanations of the characters of zhou and yi from all traditional perspectives, and then introduces the relationship between Confucius (551-479 BCE) and the later Yi zhuan (Commentaries on the Changes).

374 Pages
Paperback 978-1-63051-687-1 $32
Hardcover 978-1-63051-688-8 $75

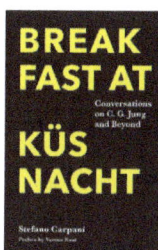

Stefano Carpani

Breakfast At Küsnacht

Conversations on C.G. Jung and Beyond

A series of interviews with 10 Jungians that begins by asking them about the central steps of their intellectual biography/journey and which authors (or research areas) they consider essential for their own development and work (also beyond psychoanalysis).

276 Pages
Paperback
978-1-63051-804-2 $32
Hardcover
978-1-63051-805-9 $49

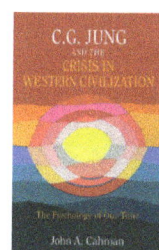

John A. Cahman

C. G. Jung and the Crisis in Western Civilization

The Psychology of Our Time

This book traces the history of Western Civilization as a developmental process and shows how our time marks a great turning point in that story as we leave an age of sexism, racism, and hierarchy and enter one of individuation.

350 Pages
Paperback
978-1-63051-764-9 $26.95
Hardcover
978-1-63051-765-6 $37

Barry Ulanov

Jung and the Outside World

Much has been written about the life and work of C.G. Jung, but little attention has been given to his impact on other modern thinkers and writers. Barry Ulanov discusses what they say—both positive and negative—about Jung's ideas and his influence on their own creative lives.

268 Pages
Paperback
978-0-93302-958-3 $21.95
Hardcover
978-1-63051-002-2 $44

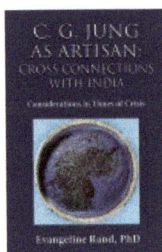

Evangeline Rand, PhD

C. G. Jung as Artisan - Cross Connections with India

Considerations in Times of Crisis

A richly illustrated, carefully interwoven tapestry of cosmological cycles with depths of travelling, trade, and commercial significance through geographical history and politics, and the spread of philosophical, religious, and scientific ideas, personally engaged.

500 Pages
Paperback 978-1-63051-964-3 $67
Hardcover 978-1-63051-965-0 $84

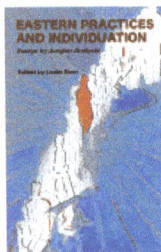

Leslie Stein

Eastern Practices and Individuation

Essays by Jungian Analysts

Eastern paths and their practices have been absorbed into Western culture. It is thus timely to approach the contemporary relevance of Eastern religions and practices to the Jungian path of individuation. Edited by Leslie Stein, these essays are personal, engaging, and contain a refined analysis of whether these two paths may work together or are pointing to different end points.

378 Pages
Paperback 978-1-68503-056-8 $32
Hardcover 978-1-68503-057-5 $45

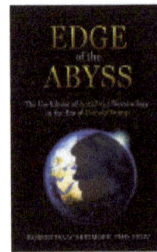

Robert Isaac Skidmore, PHD. MDIV

Edge of the Abyss

The Usefulness of Antichrist Terminology in the Era of Donald Trump

Seeing Donald Trump's cultural and political influence as expressive of an archetypal pattern, Skidmore explores implications of taking the idea of antichrist seriously—in order to lift it toward conscious awareness and responsible use.

92 Pages
Paperback 978-1-63051-895-0 $16.95
Hardcover 978-1-63051-896-7 $29

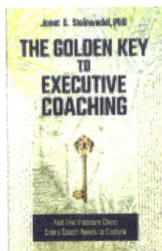

Janet S. Steinwedel, PhD

The Golden Key to Executive Coaching

And One Treasure Chest Every Coach Needs to Explore

A guide for executive coaches that also contains value for all seeking to more fully integrate their authentic selves into their professional careers.

274 Pages
Paperback
978-1-63051-351-1 $26.95
Hardcover
978-1-63051-352-8 $37

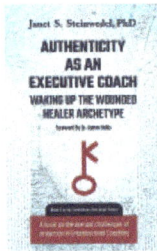

Janet S. Steinwedel, PhD

Authenticity as an Executive Coach

Waking up the Wounded Healer Archetype

In an effort to encourage more consciously engaged organizations, Janet Steinwedel brings us back to critical reflection on oneself – the Coach – and the work she or he does on her or his own inner life.

111 Pages
Paperback
978-1-63051-464-8 $18.95
Hardcover
978-1-63051-465-5 $28

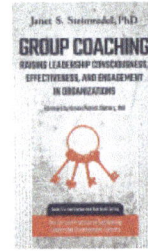

Janet S. Steinwedel, PhD

Group Coaching

Raising Leadership Consciousness, Effectiveness, and Engagement in Organizations

This is the third book in the Steinwedel Red Book Series—a series focused on the integration of Jungian psychology and executive coaching.

162 Pages
Paperback
978-1-63051-744-1 $18.95
Hardcover
978-1-63051-745-8 $27

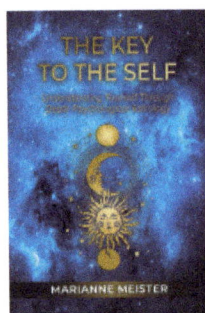

Marianne Meister

The Key to the Self

Understanding Yourself Through Depth Psychological Astrology

Our fate is NOT written in the stars, as the popular form of interpreting horoscopes would like us to believe. Instead, a serious approach to astrology describes an individual's special dispositions and developmental possibilities that can be lived out in entirely different ways. The experienced Jungian analyst and astrologer Marianne Meister connects this reputable astrological approach with the theories of C.G. Jung's Analytical Psychology.

262 Pages
Paperback
978-1-68503-048-3 $37
Hardcover
978-1-68503-049-0 $52

©2023 Chiron Publications | www.chironpublications.com

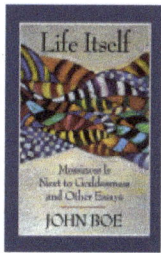

John Boe

Life Itself

Messiness Is Next to Goddessness and Other Essays

John Boe offers many delightful and personal snapshots of his humorous and often revealing approach to living. In these short, witty essays, he slices life along the lines of Jungian psychology applied to such everyday topics as holidays, palmistry, Shakespeare, movies, astrology, and more, while behind the humor is a satisfying glimpse of wisdom and experience.

180 Pages
Available in Paperback Only
978-0-93302-986-6 $21.95

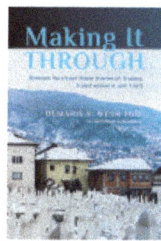

Demaris S. Wehr PHD

Making It Through

Bosnian Survivors Share Stories of Trauma, Transcendence, and Truth

Dr. Demaris Wehr came to Bosnia after the war to assist in peacebuilding trainings, and she returned several times to bear witness as survivors of the genocide told her their stories in one-on-one interviews. She asked each of them, "How did you make it through?"

204 Pages
Paperback 978-1-63051-846-2 $21.95
Hardcover 978-1-63051-847-9 $32

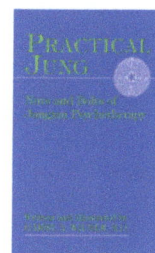

Harry A. Wilmer

Practical Jung

Nuts and Bolts of Jungian Psychology

Author Harry A. Wilmer applies his experience and wisdom to link the world of Jung with the real world. He explores complex subjects and deep theories in deceptively light style, employing his special wit and skill as a cartoonist.

296 Pages
Paperback 978-1-63051-266-8 $21.95
Hardcover 978-1-88860-277-7 $42

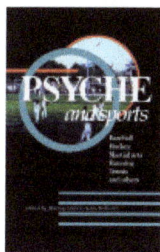

Murray Stein and John Hollwitz

Psyche and Sports

Baseball, Hockey, Martial Arts, Running, Swimming, Tennis and Others

Psyche and Sports offers a look at a variety of sports from the collective, mythical and psychological perspective, from the viewpoints of both spectators and players, in a collection that spans the history and universality of the human psyche at play.

256 Pages
Paperback 978-0-93302-979-8 $21.95
Hardcover 978-1-63051-016-9 $42

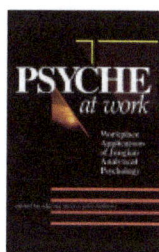

Murray Stein and John Hollwitz

Psyche at Work

Workplace Applications of Jungian Analytical Psychology

In this volume, the work of analytical psychologists, organizational development consultants, and group relations theorists reflect on the contemporary enigma presiding over an organization's unconscious.

248 Pages
Paperback 978-1-63051-245-3 $21.95
Hardcover 978-1-63051-005-3 $42

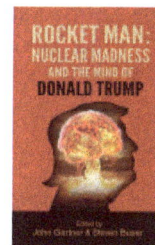

John Gartner and Steven Buser

Rocket Man

Nuclear Madness and the Mind of Donald Trump

The 24 experts who contributed to this book analyze President Trump's behavior hoping to provide insights into what may be the most urgent question of our time. What will Trump do with his "big button?"

228 Pages
Paperback 978-1-63051-588-1 $24.95
Hardcover 978-1-63051-589-8 $45

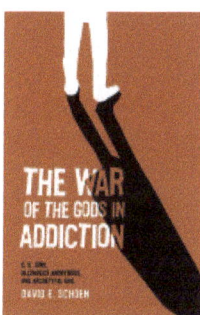

David E. Schoen

The War Of The Gods In Addiction

C.G. Jung, Alcoholics Anonymous, and Archetypal Evil

This book based on the correspondence between Bill W., one of the founders of Alcoholics Anonymous, and Swiss psychiatrist, C.G. Jung, proposes an original, groundbreaking, psychodynamic view of addiction. Using insights from Jungian psychology, it demonstrates why the twelve steps of AA really work.

176 Pages
Paperback
978-1-63051-920-9 $21.95
Hardcover
978-1-63051-921-6 $32

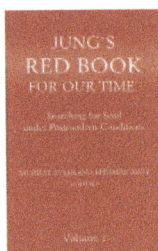

Murray Stein and Thomas Arzt

Jung`s Red Book for our Time Volume 1

Searching for Soul under Postmodern Conditions

The essays in this volume are geared to the recognition that the posthumous publication of *The Red Book: Liber Novus* by C. G. Jung in 2009 was a meaningful gift to our contemporary world.

418 Pages
Paperback 978-1-63051-477-8 $37
Hardcover 978-1-63051-478-5 $75

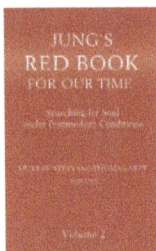

Murray Stein and Thomas Arzt

Jung`s Red Book for our Time Volume 2

Searching for Soul under Postmodern Conditions

The essays in this volume continue what was begun in Volume 1 by further contextualizing *The Red Book* culturally and interpreting it for our time.

416 Pages
Paperback 978-1-63051-578-2 $37
Hardcover 978-1-63051-579-9 $75

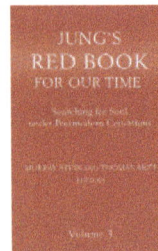

Murray Stein and Thomas Arzt

Jung's Red Book for Our Time Volume 3

Searching for Soul under Postmodern Conditions

This is the third volume of a multi-volume series set up on a global and multicultural level and includes essays from distinguished Jungian analysts and scholars.

410 Pages
Paperback 978-1-63051-716-8 $37
Hardcover 978-1-63051-717-5 $75

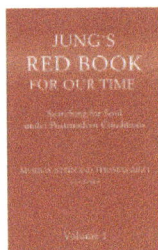

Murray Stein and Thomas Arzt

Jung`s Red Book for our Time Volume 4

Searching for Soul under Postmodern Conditions

This is the fourth volume of a multi-volume series set up on a global and multicultural level and includes essays from distinguished Jungian analysts and scholars.

416 Pages
Paperback 978-1-63051-816-5 $37
Hardcover 978-1-63051-817-2 $75

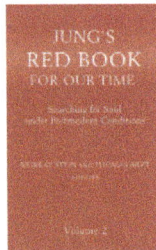

Murray Stein and Thomas Arzt

Jung`s Red Book for our Time Volume 5

Searching for Soul In the 21st Century – An Eranos Symposium

The essays contained in this fifth and final volume in the series were delivered at the Eranos Symposium on "Jung's Red Book for Our Time: Searching for Soul in the 21st Century," held at Monté Veritá Conference Center in Ascona, Switzerland on April 28 – May 1, 2022.

368 Pages
Paperback 978-1-68503-117-6 $37
Hardcover 978-1-68503-118-3 $75

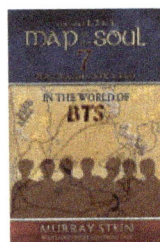

Murray Stein

Map of the Soul – 7

Persona, Shadow & Ego in the World of BTS

This book launches into a deep, engaging examination of the BTS album Map of the Soul: 7 in the light of the psychology of Jung. The many layers of meaning embedded in the number 7 are brought to light, along with several fundamental concepts of Jungian psychology.

198 Pages
Paperback 978-1-63051-850-9 $16.95
Hardcover 978-1-63051-851-6 $32

Murray Stein

Map of the Soul – 7 – French Edition

La Persona, l'Ombre et l'Ego dans le monde de BTS

BTS l'a encore fait! Map of the Soul: 7 est la pierre angulaire d'un projet de 2 albums destiné à révéler le paysage intérieur de l'âme humaine, riche en symbolisme et tissé avec le son et les mouvements caractéristiques de BTS. En commençant par les paroles, ce livre se lance dans un examen approfondi et engageant de l'album à la lumière de la psychologie jungienne.

200 Pages
Paperback 978-1-63051-912-4 $16.95
Hardcover 978-1-63051-913-1 $32

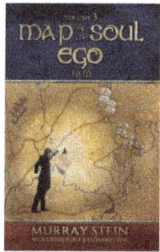

Murray Stein

Map of the Soul – Ego

I Am

In this third book in the series, *Map of the Soul – Ego: I Am*, Dr. Murray Stein explores the beginnings of consciousness and the concept of the "I," as well as the evocative lyrics from the Korean Pop band BTS's album, Map of the Soul: 7.

---

100 Pages
Paperback 978-1-63051-841-7 $14.95
Hardcover 978-1-63051-842-4 $26.95

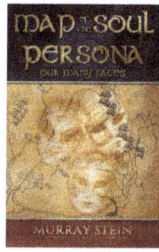

Murray Stein

Map of the Soul – Persona

Our Many Faces

What is our persona and how does it affect our life's journey? What masks do we wear as we engage those around us? Our persona is ultimately how we relate to the world. Combined with our ego, shadow, anima and other intra-psychic elements it creates an internal map of the soul.

---

116 Pages
Paperback 978-1-63051-720-5 $14.95
Hardcover 978-1-63051-721-2 $26.95

Murray Stein

Map of the Soul – Persona
Chinese Edition

在当今的文化中，有关角色角色的概念和一个人的内心世界的心理映射引起了人们极大的兴趣。实际上，人们的兴趣是如此强烈，以至于超级巨星韩国流行乐团BTS采纳了默里·斯坦因博士的概念，并将其融入了他们最新专辑 Map of the Soul : Persona的标题和歌词中。

---

102 Pages
Paperback 978-1-63051-824-0 $14.95
Hardcover 978-1-63051-825-7 $26.95

Murray Stein

Map of the Soul – Persona
Korean Edition

페르소나의 개념과 내면의 심리적 매핑에 관한 오늘날의 문화에는 많은 관심이 있습니다. 실제로 슈퍼 스타 코리아 팝 밴드 인 BTS는 머레이 스타 인 박사의 컨셉을 취해 최신 앨범 인 Map of the Soul : Persona의 제목과 가사에 엮어 놓았다.

---

144 Pages
Paperback
978-1-63051-808-0 $14.95
Hardcover
978-1-63051-809-7 $26.95

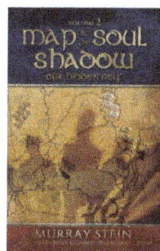

Murray Stein

Map of the Soul – Shadow

Our Hidden Self

In this second book in the series, Dr. Murray Stein explores the dark recesses of our psyche, as well as the shadow images in BTS' latest songs in their album Map of the Soul: 7.

---

140 Pages
Paperback
978-1-63051-800-4 $14.95
Hardcover
978-1-63051-801-1 $26.95

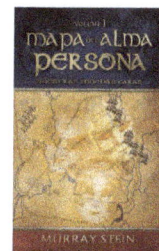

Murray Stein

Mapa Del Alma

Persona: Nuestras Muchas Caras [Map of the Soul: Persona – Spanish Edition]

Hay un gran interés en la cultura actual sobre la idea de Persona y el mapeo psicológico del mundo interior. De hecho, el interés es tan fuerte que la banda superestrella de pop coreano, BTS, ha tomado los conceptos del Dr. Murray Stein y los ha incluido en el título y la letra de su último álbum, Map of the Soul: Persona.

---

122 Pages
Paperback 978-1-63051-788-5 $14.95
Hardcover 978-1-63051-789-2 $26.95

JUNGIAN THEORY

Lena B. Ross and Manisha Roy

Cast the First Stone
Ethics in Analytical Practice

A timely and objective analysis of sexuality, power, and ethics in the relationship between analyst and analysand focusing on the symbolic attitude.

---

168 Pages
Paperback 978-0-93302-989-7 $26.95
Hardcover 978-1-63051-020-6 $42

Carlos Amadeu Botelho Byington

Creative Envy
The Rescue of One of Civilization's Major Forces

Based on Jungian Symbolic Psychology, *Creative Envy* attributes an archetypal foundation to the ego defense mechanisms of psychoanalysis and describes the possibility of all psychological functions being creative or defensive.

---

148 Pages
Paperback 978-1-88860-230-2 $14.95
Hardcover 978-1-63051-043-5 $34

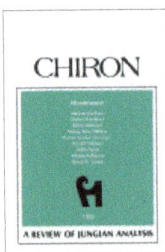

*Murray Stein and
Various Authors*

Abandonment

A Review of Jungian Analysis

Jungian theories and clinical approaches to the central therapeutic and developmental issue of abandonment are featured with topics covering early infancy, the creative woman, transformation, and others. Papers by Woodman, Fordham, Frantz, Willeford, Cornes, and others.

250 Pages
Paperback 978-1-63051-070-1 $21.95
Hardcover 978-1-88860-267-8 $42

*Robert L. Moore
Edited by Max J. Havlick, Jr.*

Facing the Dragon

Confronting Personal and Spiritual Grandiosity

Structured around a series of lectures presented at the Jung Institute of Chicago in a program entitled "Jungian Psychology and Human Spirituality: Liberation from Tribalism in Religious Life," this book-length essay attacks the related problems of human evil, spiritual narcissism, secularism and ritual, and grandiosity.

270 Pages
Paperback 978-1-88860-221-0 $21.95
Hardcover 978-1-63051-040-4 $42

*Nathan
Schwartz-Salant*

The Borderline Personality

Vision and Healing

This book offers insights into the inner life of the so-called borderline patient that are unparalleled in the psychoanalytic or Jungian literature.

256 Pages
Paperback
978-0-93302-931-6 $32
Hardcover
978-1-88860-281-4 $44.95

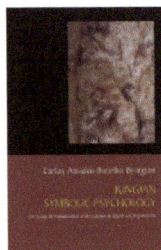

*Carlos Amadeu
Botelho Byington*

Jungian Symbolic Psychology

The Voyage of Humanization of the Cosmos in Search of Enlightenment

Carlos Amadeu Botelho Byington M.D., conceives the cultural Self and the humanization process to describe an archetypal theory of history.

386 Pages
Paperback
978-1-88860-249-4 $21.95
Hardcover
978-1-63051-065-7 $42

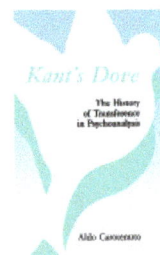

Aldo Carotenuto

Kant's Dove

The History of Transference in Psychoanalysis

Aldo Carotenuto demonstrates that the analyst cannot exclude the transference and countertransference from the analytical field—that movement toward healing is not possible without the medium of relationship, created by the interacting personalities of analyst and analysand.

182 Pages
Available in Paperback Only
978-1-63051-251-4 $21.95

*Barbara Hannah and Marie-Louise von Franz
Interviewed by Claude Drey*

Lectures on Jung's Aion

Aion, a major work from Jung's later years, has long been a source of fascination for a wide variety of scholars and thinkers. Presented here are two substantial commentaries concerning this rich and complex text by two important figures in Jung's life and work: Barbara Hannah and Marie-Louise von Franz.

234 Pages
Paperback 978-1-63051-347-4 $28
Hardcover 978-1-63051-045-9 $65

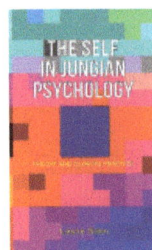

Leslie Stein

The Self in Jungian Psychology

Theory and Clinical Practice

This work synthesizes the thousands of statements Jung made about the Self in order to bring it to ground, to unravel its true purpose, and to understand how it might be able to manifest.

434 Pages
Paperback 978-1-63051-980-3 $34
Hardcover 978-1-63051-981-0 $47

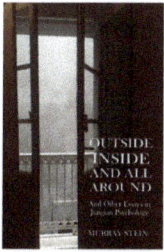

Murray Stein

Outside Inside and All Around

And Other Essays in Jungian Psychology

In these late essays, Murray Stein circles around familiar Jungian themes such as synchronicity, individuation, archetypal image and symbol with a view to bringing these ideas into today's largely globalized cultural space.

338 Pages
Paperback 978-1-63051-426-6 $32
Hardcover 978-1-63051-427-3 $75

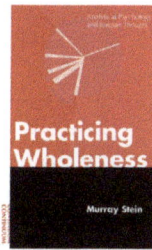

Murray Stein

Practicing Wholeness

Murray Stein argues that practicing wholeness is relevant to many areas of our lives: our private inner worlds; our religious beliefs, images, and rituals; our organizational involvements; and our cultural paradigms.

236 Pages
Paperback 978-1-63051-091-6 $21.95
Hardcover 978-1-63051-092-3 $42

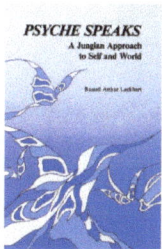

Ruddell Lockhart

Psyche Speaks

A Jungian Approach to Self and World

It is the author's sense that the failure in modern life to nurse psyche in ourselves and in others does, in fact, open the door to madness. Madness itself becomes nurse.

144 Pages
Available in Paperback Only
978-1-63051-269-9 $21.95

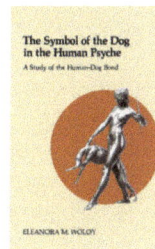

Eleanora Woloy

The Symbol of the Dog in the Human Psyche

A study of the human-dog bond and their history as companions to the human race, their roles in mythology and religion, and their appearance in dreams.

104 Pages
Paperback 978-0-93302-947-7 $21.95
Hardcover 978-1-88860-292-0 $32

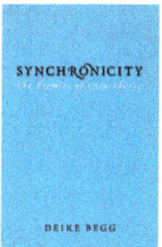

Deike Begg

Synchronicity

The Promise of Coincidence

Deike Begg explores synchronicity as signposts and the universe's call of destiny. She describes in clear language how to recognize a synchronicity: i.e. if it is not an emotional response to the intersection of two different sorts of time or worlds it is not a synchronicity.

160 Pages
Paperback 978-1-88860-231-9 $21.95
Hardcover 978-1-63051-046-6 $32

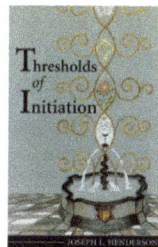

Joseph L. Henderson

Thresholds of Initiation

Joseph Henderson considers archetypes to be predictable patterns of inner conditioning that lead to certain essential changes and shows the parallels between individual psychological self-development and the rites that marked initiation in the past.

288 Pages
Paperback 978-1-63051-224-8 $24.95
Hardcover 978-1-63051-048-0 $44

Harry A. Wilmer

Understandable Jung

The Personal Side of Jungian Psychology

This sequel to *Practical Jung* offers humorous anecdotes and a wealth of useful information for teachers, therapists, social workers, pastoral counselors, and anyone who has ever wanted to know or understand more about Jungian ideas.

296 Pages
Paperback 978-0-93302-969-9 $32
Hardcover 978-1-63051-018-3 $44.95

JUNGIAN THERAPY & ANALYSIS

Michael Eigen

Coming Through the Whirlwind

Case Studies in Psychotherapy

The pain and rewards of depth therapy revealed in two case studies.

272 Pages
Paperback 978-1-63051-250-7 $21.95
Hardcover 978-1-88860-293-7 $42

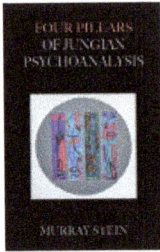

Murray Stein

The Four Pillars of Jungian Psychoanalysis

The Four Pillars of Jungian Psycho-analysis is a work that describes the methods that in combination sets this form of psychotherapy apart from all the others.

140 Pages
Paperback
978-1-68503-025-4 $27
Hardcover
978-1-68503-026-1 $39

Elie Humbert

C. G. Jung

The Fundamentals of Theory and Practice

An outstanding introduction to the spirit and practice of Jungian psychology. Analyzed by Jung, Humbert brings a unique understanding of Jung's ideas, developed over many years within the atmosphere of French psychoanalytic thought.

168 Pages
Paperback
978-0-93302-918-7 $14.95
Hardcover
978-1-88860-279-1 $42

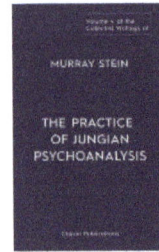

Nathan Schwartz-Salant

The Collected Writings of Murray Stein Volume 4

The Practice of Jungian Psychoanalysis

This is a practical volume, indispensable for Jungian analysts, Jungian psycho-therapists or students hoping to sharpen their analytical skills. It is truly the "nuts and bolts" of Jungian analytical practice.

460 Pages
Paperback 978-1-68503-035-3 $37
Hardcover 978-1-68503-036-0 $75

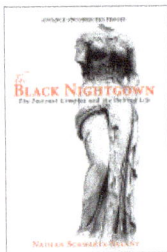

Nathan Schwartz-Salant

The Black Nightgown

The Fusional Complex and the Unlived Life

Through the cultural and individual examples of *The Black Nightgown*, the reader will see that the Fusional Complex is the doorway through which any new form of consciousness and associated self—the structure that bestows a sense of identity and order within human life—must pass.

272 Pages
Paperback 978-1-63051-223-1 $32
Hardcover 978-1-63051-054-1 $44.95

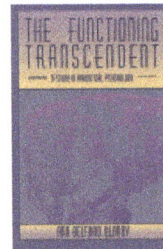

Ann Belford Ulanov

The Functioning Transcendent

A Study in Analytical Psychology

The Transcendent is the bridge between the rational and irrational, the conscious and unconscious. Ann Belford Ulanov demonstrates the reality of the Transcendent through ten examples taken from her years of practice as a Jungian analyst.

232 Pages
Paperback 978-0-93302-999-6 $32
Hardcover 978-1-63051-025-1 $44.95

Aldo Carotenuto

The Difficult Art

A Critical Discourse on Psychotherapy

In a frenetic society that has given up dreams and fantasy, that is characterized by people rushing vertiginously ahead, like guinea pigs continually bombarded with stimuli rushing madly around their cage, the analyst's task is to recover the imaginary, the poetry of the soul, of the psyche.

314 Pages
Available in Paperback Only
978-0-93302-964-4 $24.95

Gunilla Midbøe

The Elliptical Dialogue

A Communications Model for Psychotherapy

The Elliptical Dialogue is presented in this book as a model for communication, dialogue and reciprocal relationship in analytical work, psychotherapy and supervision.

204 Pages
Paperback 978-1-63051-417-4 $28
Hardcover 978-1-63051-418-1 $65

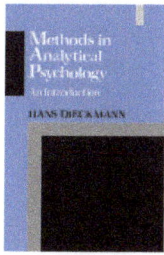

Hans Dieckmann

Methods in Analytical Psychology
An Introduction

Designed for both the beginner and the experienced clinician, this book serves as a reference for the basic methodological problems encountered in the practice of Jungian psychology.

240 Pages
Paperback 978-0-93302-948-4 $42
Hardcover 978-1-88860-297-5 $60

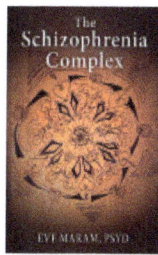

Eve Maram, PSYD

The Schizophrenia Complex

This book focuses on the thoughts and feelings constellated by encounters with what we call schizophrenia, for those who experience symptoms, and for those others impacted by them. To do so, Dr. Maram had to face her own fear, denial, resistance, and ultimate not knowing.

190 Pages
Paperback 978-1-68503-060-5 $27
Hardcover 978-1-68503-061-2 $39

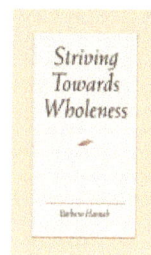

Barbara Hannah

Striving Towards Wholeness

Barbara Hannah studies the psychic processes that move people to strive for wholeness of personality, an integration of all innate capacities.

328 Pages
Paperback 978-1-88860-213-5 $27.95
Hardcover 978-1-63051-036-7 $44

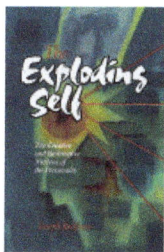

Joseph Redfearn

The Exploding Self
The Creative and Destructive Nucleus of the Personality

Creative regression, living closer to one's fundamental nature, is what we are learning about today. But how to apply our knowledge on a world scale so as collectively to avoid violent swings and explosions is, of course, an unsolved problem of our era of massive blindness and consequent mass behaviors.

312 Pages
Paperback 978-0-93302-960-6 $27.95
Hardcover 978-1-63051-001-5 $34

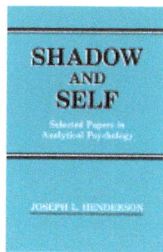

Joseph Henderson

Shadow and Self
Selected Papers in Analytical Psychology

Joseph L. Henderson's first formulations of previously discussed theories, as well as issues related to these centers of his thinking and his work. These papers are derived from his clinical practice and his cross-disciplinary investigations of chosen aspects of culture.

346 Pages
Paperback 978-0-93302-933-0 $32
Hardcover 978-1-88860-291-3 $42

Marianne Tauber

The Soul's Ministrations
An Imaginal Journey through Crisis

When her husband was diagnosed with a serious brain tumor, Marianne Tauber turned to art—painting and poetry—to cope with the situation. Years later, she explicates what was behind the drive to create, presenting seventeen paintings and poems alongside a narrative of the time of crisis in journal form.

168 Pages
Available in Paperback Only
978-1-88860-254-8 $26.95

Daniel A. Lindley

On Life's Journey
Always Becoming

In this reflection on life's journey, Daniel Lindley applies the insights gleaned from many years of study of literature and psychoanalysis to show how we are *always becoming* and always obligated to care for that archetypal child.

172 Pages
Paperback 978-1-63051-255-2 $21.95
Hardcover 978-1-88860-240-1 $42

Laura Dodson and Terrill Gibson

Psyche and Family
Jungian Applications to Family Therapy

This combination of Jungian analysis and family therapy gives both systems the opportunity to further their combined mission toward health and wholeness.

176 Pages
Paperback 978-1-88860-202-9 $26.95
Hardcover 978-1-63051-027-5 $65

Emmett Early

The Raven's Return
The Influence of Psychological Trauma on Individuals and Culture

An insightful look at post-traumatic stress disorder by a former counselor of Vietnam veterans.

152 Pages
Available in Paperback Only
978-0-93302-970-5 $21.95

KOA BOOKS

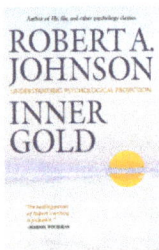

Robert A. Johnson

Inner Gold

Understanding Psychological Projection

Robert A. Johnson shares a lifetime of insights and experiences in this easy-to-read book on psychological projection—seeing traits in others that are, in fact, our own.

88 Pages
Available in Paperback Only
978-0-9821656-6-9 $16.95

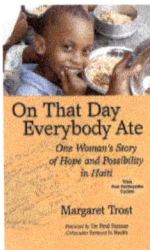

Margaret Trost

On That Day, Everybody Ate

One Woman's Story of Hope and Possibility in Haiti

Following her husband's untimely death, Margaret Trost visited Haiti to heal her broken heart through service. This book is an autobiography of her remarkable journey.

168 Pages
Available in Paperback Only
978-0-98216-569-0 $16.95

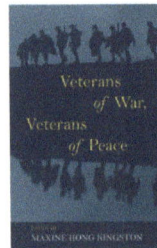

Maxine Hong Kingston

Veterans of War, Veterans of Peace

This poignant collection, compiled from Kingston's healing workshops, contains the distilled wisdom of survivors of five wars, including combatants, war widows, spouses, children, conscientious objectors, and veterans of domestic abuse.

624 Pages
Available in Paperback Only
978-1-93564-623-5 $26.95

Cindy Sheehan

Not One More Mother's Child

Cindy Sheehan lost her son, Spc. Casey Austin Sheehan, in an ambush in Sadr City, Baghdad, in early 2004. *Not One More Mother's Child* tells in her distinctive voice how historical events and personal tragedy transformed her from grieving mom to ardent activist.

234 Pages
Available in Paperback Only
978-1-93564-626-6 $16.95

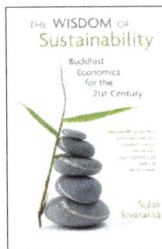

Sulak Sivaraksa

The Wisdom of Sustainability

Buddhist Economics for the 21st Century

This book continues E. F. Schumacher's groundbreaking work on Buddhist economics in *Small Is Beautiful: Economics as if People Mattered*. Emphasizing small-scale, indigenous, sustainable alternatives to globalization, Sulak offers hope and alternatives for restructuring our economies based on Buddhist principles and personal development.

114 Pages
Available in Paperback Only
978-1-93564-614-3 $21.95

Koohan Paik and Jerry Mander

The Superferry Chronicles

Hawaii's Uprising Against Militarism, Commercialism, and the Desecration of the Earth

This book is a riveting tale of intrigue and corruption—and an inspiring popular uprising against rampant commercialization.

330 Pages
Available in Paperback Only
978-1-93564-617-4 $21.95

Lama Surya Das

Words of Wisdom

A rich tapestry of insight gems and belly laughs, *Words of Wisdom* will leave you laughing, searching your soul, and asking for more. Each page contains a statement that focuses the reader's attention on an essential concept. An ideal gift book & wisdom treasure for seekers of all faiths.

154 Pages
Available in Paperback Only
978-1-93564-620-4 $11.95

MEN & THE MASCULINE

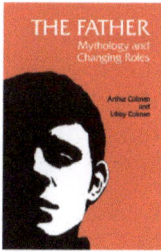

Arthur Colman

The Father

Mythology and Changing Roles

The Father: Mythology and Changing Roles examines the changing role of the father in today's family and explores the impact of fatherhood on a man's life.

228 Pages
Paperback
978-0-93302-935-4 $26.95
Hardcover
978-1-88860-280-7 $37.95

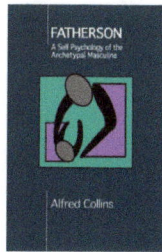

Alfred Collins

Fatherson

A Self Psychology of the Archetypal Masculine

Using a varied palate of examples from the literature of both Western and non-Western cultures, Alfred Collins illustrates the Fatherson archetype from angles both personal and professional.

170 Pages
Paperback
978-0-93302-975-0 $16.95
Hardcover
978-1-63051-009-1 $42

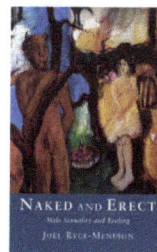

Joel Ryce-Menuhin

Naked and Erect

Male Sexuality and Feeling

In this frank and honest airing of male sexuality, Jungian analyst Joel Ryce-Menuhin presents a rare comprehension of the male experience gathered from over 20 years of working with male clients. By presenting male sexuality along with its psychological and spiritual issues, his work adds to our understanding of men today.

160 Pages
Paperback 978-1-88860-200-5 $14.95
Hardcover 978-1-63051-069-5 $42

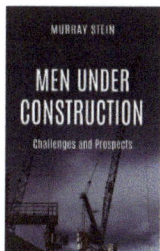

Murray Stein

Men Under Construction

Challenges and Prospects

In these lectures Murray Stein describes five "eras" or stages in a lifelong process of psychological and spiritual growth, as well as speaking about friendship between men and the archetypal gestures of fathering. The lectures are intended to help men of all ages to orient themselves in their lives as they search for meaning and seek personal development.

150 Pages
Paperback 978-1-63051-792-2 $26.95
Hardcover 978-1-63051-793-9 $47

Murray Stein

Konstruktion Mann

Herausforderungen und Perspektiven
[Men Under Construction – German Edition]

In den hier versammelten Vorträgen beschreibt Murray Stein fünf "Stadien" oder Stufen in einem lebenslangen Prozess des psychologischen und spirituellen Wachstums und spricht auch über die Freundschaft zwischen Männern und die archetypischen Gesten des Bevaterns. Die Vorträge sollen Männern jeden Alters helfen, sich in ihrem Leben auf der Suche nach Sinn und persönlicher Entwicklung zu orientieren.

180 Pages
Paperback 978-1-63051-866-0 $26.95
Hardcover 978-1-63051-867-7 $47

MYTHOLOGY

Pierre Solié

Mythanalysis

Mythographer and psychologist Pierre Solié pays particular attention to two myths about the Great Mother—those pertaining to the Babylonian goddess Tiamat and the Egyptian goddess Isis. Numerous clinical cases are also presented that support the use of myth in therapy.

128 Pages
Available only in Paperback
978-1-88860-203-6 $14.95

Barbara Hannah

The Archetypal Symbolism of Animals

Barbara Hannah, a student and a close friend of C.G. Jung, presents lectures on the symbolic meaning of several domestic and wild animals. According to Jung, the animal is sublime and, in fact, represents the divine side of the human psyche.

430 Pages
Paperback
978-1-63051-074-9 $32
Hardcover
978-1-63051-049-7 $44.95

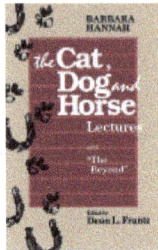

Barbara Hannah

The Cat, Dog and Horse Lectures, and The Beyond

Toward the Development of Human Conscious

This book features a seminar given at the Psychological Club in 1954 about the images of the cat, the dog, and the horse in the psychological and cultural life of the western world.

152 Pages
Paperback 978-0-93302-959-0 $21.95
Hardcover 978-1-63051-000-8 $42

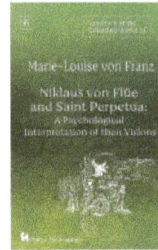

Marie-Louise von Franz

Collected Works of Marie-Louise von Franz Volume 6

Niklaus Von Flüe and Saint Perpetua: A Psychological Interpretation of their Visions

This volume heralds translations of material never before available in English. It explores the profound visions of two ground-breaking saints in the Catholic church, Saint Niklaus von Flüe and Saint Perpetua.

244 Pages
Paperback 978-1-68503-029-2 $37
Hardcover 978-1-68503-030-8 $57

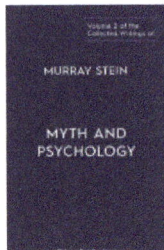

Murray Stein

Collected Writings of Murray Stein Volume 2

Myth and Psychology

Volume 2 looks at Mythology through a Jungian lens. Dr. Stein examines a vast array of mythologic figures. Mythology is ripe with transformative symbols reaching deep into our unconscious.

268 Pages
Paperback 978-1-63051-871-4 $37
Hardcover 978-1-63051-872-1 $75

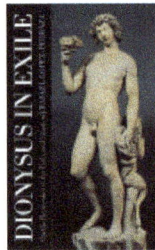

Rafael Lopez-Pedraza

Dionysus in Exile

On the Repression of the Body and Emotion

Lopez-Pedraza diagnoses the psychological illness at the core of modern society–the loss of embodied soulfulness in people's lives. In this study of the Greek god Dionysus, he offers insight for a cure.

114 Pages
Paperback 978-1-88860-210-4 $21.95
Hardcover 978-1-63051-033-6 $42

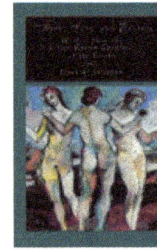

John A. Sanford

Fate, Love and Ecstasy

Wisdom from the Lesser-Known Goddesses of the Greeks

In this book, John Sanford turns his attention to the lesser-known goddesses seldom mentioned in Jungian literature.

136 Pages
Paperback 978-1-63051-323-8 $21.95
Hardcover 978-0-93302-996-5 $42

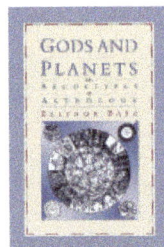

Ellynor Barz

Gods and Planets

The Archetypes of Astrology

Drawing on the psychology of Jung, Ellynor Barz looks into the foundations of astrology by recounting the myths of the planetary gods. Engaging and amusing, her presentation also offers new and surprising insights for both psychology and astrology.

216 Pages
Available in Paperback Only
Paperback 978-0-93302-971-2 $14.95

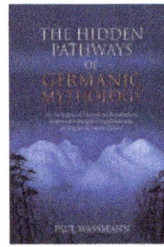

Paul Wassmann

The Hidden Pathways of Germanic Mythology

On the Neglected, Demonized, Repulsed and Repressed Archetypical Representations of Original Germanic Culture

This book offers an overview of the hidden pathways of Germanic Mythology, focusing upon the Germanic Word View, the creation of the world, the Dawn of Gods and the psychological role of some of the most significant gods and goddesses.

268 Pages
Paperback 978-1-63051-712-0 $32
Hardcover 978-1-63051-713-7 $47

Arlene Diane Landau

Tragic Beauty

The Dark Side of Venus Aphrodite and the Loss and Regeneration of Soul

Aphrodite women always stand out. In these times, when the idolization of Aphrodite—and the tragedy that ensues—are perhaps more widespread than ever, the crucial key for women is consciousness.

118 Pages
Paperback 978-1-63051-776-2 $24.95
Hardcover 978-1-63051-777-9 $34

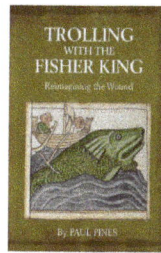

Paul Pines

Trolling with the Fisher King

Reimagining the Wound

As a fisherman/seaman touched by war zones and wastelands in Viet Nam and the Bowery, a poet/therapist who has worked with his own wounds, and those of others, author Paul Pines believes that the Fisher King's wounding can be understood as a function that speaks to our post-internet condition on the border of survival and extinction.

172 Pages
Paperback 978-1-63051-459-4 $26.95
Hardcover 978-1-63051-460-0 $37

PHILOSOPHY & SOCIAL THEORY

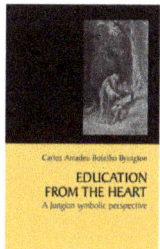

Carlos Amadeu Botelho Byington

Education from the Heart

A Jungian Symbolic Perspective

Jungian symbolic education takes as its model life and life's natural ways of teaching. Its foundation is Carlos Byington's theory of Jungian symbolic psychology, which describes archetypal patterns of consciousness by elaborating symbols coordinated by archetypes.

355 Pages
Paperback 978-1-88860-248-7 $14.95
Hardcover 978-1-63051-058-9 $44

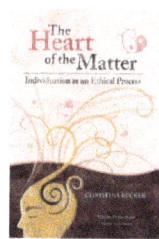

Christina Becker

The Heart of the Matter

Individuation as an Ethical Process

Christina Becker takes the reader through the philosophical and spiritual aspects of the ethical dimensions of an individual journey toward wholeness.

188 Pages
Paperback 978-1-63051-071-8 $21.95
Hardcover 978-1-63051-072-5 $42

Vera Buhrmann

Living in Two Worlds

Communication Between a White Healer and Her Black Counterparts

Living in Two Worlds is required reading for anyone interested in the social, political and psychological realities of southern Africa.

114 Pages
Available in Paperback Only
978-0-93302-910-1 $21.95

Theodor Abt

Progress Without Loss of Soul

Toward a Wholistic Approach to Modernization Planning

Dr. Theodor Abt has made an important contribution toward articulating a holistic approach to the process of planning for modernization. He has touched upon some of the deeper issues involved which require our careful and sustained attention.

416 Pages
Paperback 978-1-63051-256-9 $28
Hardcover 978-0-93302-936-1 $65

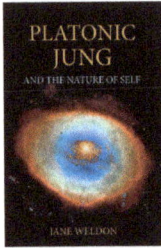

Jane Weldon

Platonic Jung and the Nature of Self

The Platonic Jung re-unites philosophy and psychology and expresses the message Jung and Plato imparted to the world; that the soul is the true self, and is worth finding.

260 Pages
Paperback
978-1-63051-401-3 $28
Hardcover
978-1-63051-402-0 $65

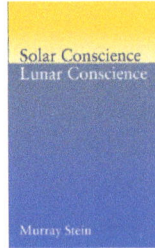

Murray Stein

Solar Conscience/Lunar Conscience

The Psychological Foundations of Morality, Lawfulness, and the Sense of Justice

Murray Stein explores the origins and work of conscience. Using the myths of Orestes and Prometheus as examples, he defines solar conscience as an inner voice that represents the values of society, and lunar conscience as an instinctive inner sense which seeks to fulfill underlying qualities of right and wrong.

144 Pages
Paperback 978-1-63051-268-2 $21.95
Hardcover 978-1-63051-011-4 $32

Karla Andersdatter

The Woman Who Was Wild

Inimitably told by renowned storyteller Karla Andersdatter, this collection of tales comes with a commentary by Jungian analyst C.E. Brookes. Concentrating on lost goddesses, love, and healing our environment, the author offers poignant observations about the world in which we live and the disappearance of loving values from it.

176 Pages
Available in Paperback Only
978-0-93302-976-7 $21.95

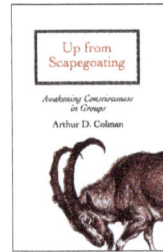

Arthur D. Colman

Up from Scapegoating

Awakening Consciousness in Groups

Many groups defend themselves against the different, the new, and the perceived negative, by collectively rejecting this element through the creation of a scapegoat. To accommodate diversity, Arthur Colman explores ways individuals and groups can grow beyond the continual theme of scapegoating.

168 Pages
Paperback 978-0-93302-995-8 $26.95
Hardcover 978-1-63051-024-4 $37.95

REFERENCE

Elizabeth Caspari with Ken Robbins

Animal Life in Nature, Myth and Dreams

Elizabeth Caspari connects the world of real, living animals with the symbolic world of animal images in human thought, both conscious and unconscious. She gives the reader an opportunity to make this connection on his or her own personal journey of discovery.

336 Pages
Available in Hardcover Only
978-1-88860-222-7 $65

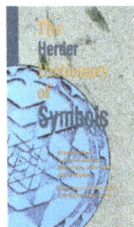

The Herder Dictionary of Symbols

In handy pocket size, this title is of great assistance to anyone interested in dream interpretation, understanding symbolism in religion and art, and the overlapping meanings of symbols from different cultures. Beautifully produced and authoritative, this detailed survey reveals an abundance of types of human symbolic thinking.

228 Pages
Available in Paperback Only
978-0-93302-984-2 $21.95

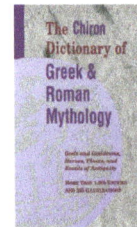

The Chiron Dictionary of Greek and Roman Mythology

A pocket guide presenting concise information on the mythology of Greek and Roman cultures from Abdera to Zeuxippe, including gods, goddesses, heroes, kings and queens. Over 270 line drawings and charts enliven the margins and provide information on the cultural representations of these mythic figures throughout history.

320 Pages
Available in Paperback Only
978-0-93302-982-8 $16.95

RELATIONSHIPS

John A. Desteian

Coming Together – Coming Apart

The Play of Opposites in Love Relationships

Relationships are hard enough to negotiate without advice from outsiders who don't know you at all. This book is not a "how-to" aimed at attaining the ideal. Rather, it is a how-it-is, an exploration of how relationships are, how they develop, how they deteriorate, how they may end and how they may even revive.

258 pages
Paperback 978-1-63051-946-9 $29
Hardcover 978-1-63051-947-6 $42

Verena Kast

Father-Daughter, Mother-Son

Freeing Ourselves from the Complexes That Bind Us

Verena Kast's *Father-Daughter, Mother-Son* was first published by Element Books in 1997. Since then, it has become a classic read for those adventuring into Carl Gustav Jung's concept of complexes—what they are, how they affect our life and shape our relationships— and for those wanting to understand more about the relationship between fathers and daughters, and mothers and sons—of whatever sex and gender.

196 Pages
Paperback 978-1-68503-072-8 $27
Hardcover 978-1-68503-073-5 $39

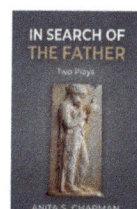

Anita S. Chapman

In Search of the Father

Two Plays

Where inadequate or incompetent fathering is combined with absent or passive, silent mothering, the balance is off; a daughter's talents and possibilities for the future can remain dormant—or fade away in self-doubt.

190 Pages
Paperback
978-1-68503-052-0 $27
Hardcover
978-1-68503-053-7 $39

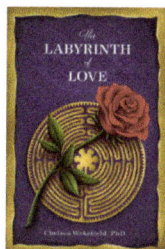

Chelsea Wakerfield, PhD

The Labyrinth of Love

The Path to a Soulful Relationship

A helpful and enlightening guidebook from an expert couples therapist that demystifies the challenges of love, then teaches us about six "love capacities" any couple can develop to set them on the path of a soulful, enduring relationship.

294 Pages
Paperback 978-1-63051-952-0 $21.95
Hardcover 978-1-63051-953-7 $34

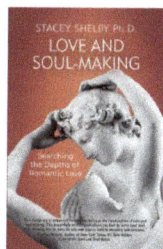

Stacey Shelby Ph.D

Love and Soul-Making

Searching the Depths of Romantic Love

This book brings awareness to both the patriarchal origins of romance and the unarguably magical, archetypal experience of love. Relationships can serve as an alchemical vessel for the development of the soul as part of the individuation process.

224 Pages
Paperback 978-1-68503-039-1 $19.95
Hardcover 978-1-68503-040-7 $37

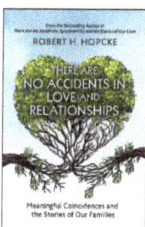

Robert H. Hopcke

There Are No Accidents in Love & Relationships

Meaningful Coincidences and the Stories of Our Families

This book focuses on family stories—how people met the love of their life, striking coincidences that are shared between siblings, parents and ancestors, ways in which synchronistic events accompany us in our transitions throughout our family histories—in order to explore both the nature of Jung's notion of synchronicity but further to illustrate how our notion and experience of "family" is fundamentally archetypal and psychological in nature, rather than merely biological or social-cultural.

218 Pages
Paperback 978-1-63051-488-4 $21.95
Hardcover 978-1-63051-489-1 $32

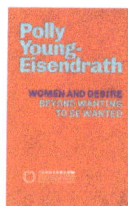

Polly Young-Eisendrath

Women and Desire: Beyond Wanting to Be Wanted

Polly Young-Eisendrath´s Women and Desire: Beyond Wanting to Be Wanted was first published by Harmony Books in 1999. Since then, it has become a classic read for those readers– to use a cinematographic expression – who want to use analytical psychology to shed light on what women want. This book, when first published, was described (and still is) as "provocative and vital."

288 Pages
Paperback 978-1-68503-121-3 $30
Hardcover 978-1-68503-122-0 $44

RELIGION & SPIRITUALITY

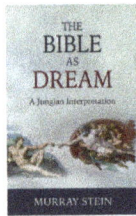

Murray Stein

The Bible as Dream

A Jungian Interpretation

Murray Stein shares these timeless lectures—a work of respectful and loving interpretation. The Bible is a dream that tells the story of how this world was brought into being in space and time and what it means.

210 Pages
Paperback
978-1-63051-668-0 $26.95
Hardcover
978-1-63051-669-7 $47

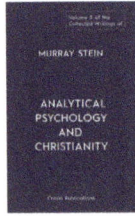

Murray Stein

Collected Writings of Murray Stein Volume 5

Analytical Psychology and Christianity

In this volume, Murray Stein illuminates Jung's relationship with Christianity and how he strove to restore its transcendent symbols.

360 Pages
Paperback 978-1-68503-137-4 $37
Hardcover 978-1-68503-138-1 $75

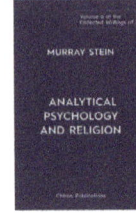

Murray Stein

Collected Writings of Murray Stein Volume 6

Analytical Psychology and Religion

This volume continues where Volume 5 left off-the archetypal exploration of religion in general and Christianity in particular, asking what it might look like if we interpreted the Christian Bible as if it were a dream.

344 Pages
Paperback 978-1-68503-084-1 $37
Hardcover 978-1-68503-085-8 $75

Murray Stein

Jung's Treatment of Christianity

The Psychotherapy of a Religious Tradition

An insightful and convincing interpretation of Jung's encounter with Christianity. Murray Stein provides a comprehensive analysis of Jung's writings on Christianity in relation to his personal life, psychological thought, and efforts to transform Western religion.

216 Pages
Paperback 978-1-63051-267-5 $28
Hardcover 978-1-88860-268-5 $65

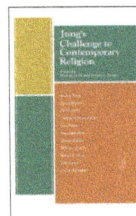

Murray Stein and Robert Moore

Jung's Challenge to Contemporary Religion

Highlights of this book include studies of the way in which Christianity is changing, the feminine dimension of God, and Jung's contribution to biblical humanities.

190 Pages
Paperback
978-1-63051-253-8 $26.95
Hardcover
978-1-88860-276-0 $42

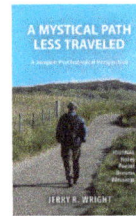

Jerry R. Wright

A Mystical Path Less Traveled

A Jungian Psychological Perspective – Journal Notes, Poems, Dreams, and Blessings

Drawing on the Analytical Psychology of Jung, on the discoveries of modern science, and on mystical traditions from numerous world religions, this book proposes a psychological mysticism that preceded, and now replaces, the historical theological mysticism that has been dependent on theistic images of god.

202 Pages
Paperback 978-1-63051-937-7 $17.95
Hardcover 978-1-63051-938-4 $29

Phyllis Moore

No Other Gods

An Interpretation of the Biblical Myth for a Transbiblical Age

No Other Gods is a wide-ranging analysis of the biblical myth of God and of its impact on culture and human consciousness, from the perspective of the evolution of consciousness that precedes and postdates it.

216 Pages
Paperback 978-1-63051-076-3 $26.95
Hardcover 978-1-63051-004-6 $37.95

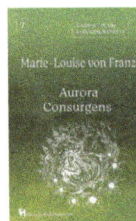

Collected Works of Marie-Louise von Franz Volume 7
Aurora Consurgens

Aurora Consurgens, the rising sun, is a vision forged in the pseudo-Aristotelian tradition that became a cornerstone of medieval Church doctrine and the centerpiece of the Dominican and Franciscan traditions. While its authorship has been shrouded in mystery and controversy, Marie-Louise von Franz furnishes ample evidence that this was a final work of Thomas Aquinas.

576 Pages
Paperback 978-1-63051-962-9 $52
Hardcover 978-1-63051-963-6 $77

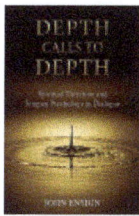

John Ensign

Depth Calls to Depth

Spiritual Direction and Jungian Psychology in Dialogue

This book draws on the author's dual background as a certified Jungian analyst and psychologist as well as a spiritual director with a master's degree in theology.

---

380 Pages
Paperback 978-1-68503-133-6 $32
Hardcover 978-1-68503-134-3 $45

Julienne Mclean

The Diamond Heart

Jungian Psychology and the Christian Mystical Tradition

Two towering figures thread their way through this book: St Teresa of Avila, the sixteenth century Spanish Carmelite saint, writer and reformer and C.G. Jung, the founder of modern depth psychology. Julienne McLean draws on their writings to focus on, and explore, the interface and relationship between the Christian mystical tradition and Jungian, depth psychology.

---

278 Pages
Paperback 978-1-68503-095-7 $27
Hardcover 978-1-68503-096-4 $42

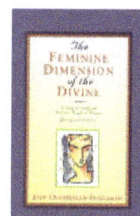

Joan Chamberlain Englesman

The Feminine Dimension of the Divine

A Study of Sophia and Feminine Images in Religion

Departing from the traditional image of God as masculine, Joan Chamberlain Engelsman examines the feminine dimension of the divine.

---

222 Pages
Paperback
978-1-63051-211-8 $19.95
Hardcover
978-1-88860-275-3 $34

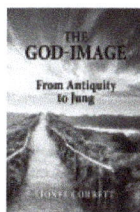

Lionel Corbett

The God-Image

From Antiquity to Jung

This book describes the development of images of God, beginning in antiquity and culminating in Jung's notion of the Self, an image of God in the psyche that Jung calls the God within.

---

530 Pages
Paperback 978-1-63051-984-1 $34
Hardcover 978-1-63051-985-8 $49

Lionel Corbett

The Sacred Cauldron

Psychotherapy as a Spiritual Practice

At a time when psychotherapy seems to be a purely secular pursuit with no connection to the sacred, *The Sacred Cauldron* makes the startling claim that, for both participants, psychotherapeutic work is actually a spiritual discipline in its own right. This book demonstrates some of the ways in which a spiritual sensibility can inform the technical aspects of psychotherapy.

---

336 Pages
Paperback 978-1-63051-275-0 $24.95
Hardcover 978-1-88860-265-4 $37.95

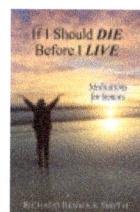

Richard Renwick Smyth

If I Should Die Before I Live

Meditations for Seniors

A disquieting question persists: "What if I should die before I feel life is full?" Spiritual experience makes promise and mystery real; this enhances earthly achievements.

---

240 Pages
Paperback
978-1-63051-473-0 $16.95
Hardcover
978-1-63051-474-7 $26.95

Bettina L. Knapp

Manna and Mystery

A Jungian Approach to Hebrew Myth and Legend

In this study, Bettina L. Knapp probes myths—such as the Golem, Dybbuk, and the *divine child*. She argues powerfully and persuasively for their relevance to believers of all religions today as they were to the Jews of the past.

---

184 Pages
Paperback 978-0-93302-980-4 $14.95
Hardcover 978-1-63051-015-2 $42

Avis Clendenen

Spirituality in Depth

Essays in Honor of Sister Irene Dugan, r.c.

Reflects the in-depth influence of a spiritual animator whose lifework was dedicated to exploring the provocative and mysterious journey of the magnitude of the inner world and its workings.

---

176 Pages
Paperback 978-1-88860-220-3 $21.95
Hardcover 978-1-63051-038-1 $32

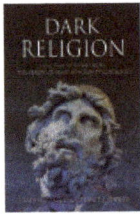

*Vladislav Šolc &
George J. Didier*

Dark Religion

**Fundamentalism From The
Perspective of Jungian Psychology**

Jungian analysts Vlado Šolc and George Didier set out to explore the psychological dynamics and causes of religious fundamentalism and fanaticism. The book reveals that spirituality is an inherent dimension and one of the most essential human needs. It only becomes "dark" when it ignores or separates itself from its own vital roots.

**454 Pages
Paperback 978-1-63051-398-6 $34
Hardcover 978-1-63051-399-3 $49**

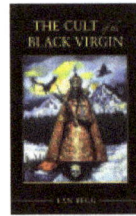

Ean Begg

The Cult of the Black Virgin

**A Jungian Psychological Perspective
– Journal Notes, Poems, Dreams,
and Blessings**

Ean Begg's fascinating book investigates the pagan origins of the phenomenon as well as the heretical Gnostic-Christian underground stream that flowed west with the cult of Mary Magdalene and resurfaced in Catharism at the time of the Crusades, especially with the Templars.

**192 Pages
Paperback 978-1-63051-270-5 $19.95
Hardcover 978-1-63051-051-0 $42**

Peter B. Todd

The Individuation of God

Integrating Science and Religion

Peter B. Todd argues for the integration of science and religion to form a new paradigm for the third millennium. Drawing on the work of scientists, psychologists, philosophers, and theologians.

**192 Pages
Paperback
978-1-88860-255-5 $21.95
Hardcover
978-1-63051-064-0 $37.95**

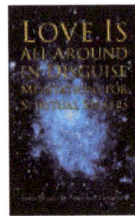

*Sr. Irene Dugan,
Avis Clendenen
and Jerri Greer*

Love Is All Around in Disguise

Meditations for Spiritual Seekers

This book—part polemic, part instruction manual—is the summation of Irene's life work, told in her own words and supported by the rich understanding of her trustee.

**210 Pages
Available in Paperback Only
978-1-88860-229-6 $14.95**

Edward F. Edinger

The New God Image

A Study of Jung's Key Letters Concerning the Evolution of the Western God-Image

Edward F. Edinger discusses fourteen of Jung's letters with respect to the epistemological premises—modern man's new awareness of subjectivity, the paradoxical God, the nature of the new God–image as a union of opposites, and the continuing incarnation, or how the new God-image is born in individual men and women.

**228 Pages
Paperback 978-1-63051-277-4 $24.95
Hardcover 978-1-63051-026-8 $44**

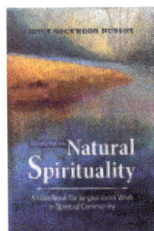

Joyce Hudson

Natural Spirituality

**A Handbook for Jungian Inner Work in Spiritual Community –
Revised Edition**

Joyce Rockwood Hudson moves Jungian dream work from the professional world of the analyst's office into the everyday world of spiritual seekers in local community, both inside and outside the institutions of traditional religion.

**408 Pages
Paperback 978-1-63051-392-4 $18.95
Hardcover 978-1-63051-393-1 $32**

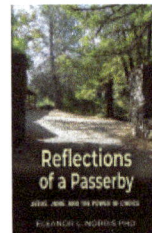

Eleanor L. Norris PHD

Reflections of a Passerby

Jesus, Jung, and the Power of Choice

Eleanor Norris, PhD, takes us along on her search for meaning through the study of the life of Jesus—the Christian myth. Was Jesus solely human or solely divine? Was he the symbol of the Self, as C.G. Jung proposed?

**328 Pages
Paperback 978-1-68503-001-8 $29
Hardcover 978-1-68503-002-5 $44**

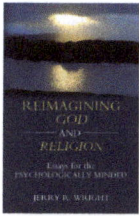

Jerry R. Wright

Reimagining God and Religion

Essays for the Psychologically Minded

Drawing on the insights of Jungian or analytical psychology, Dr. Wright offers depth psychological analysis of our contemporary religious and political dilemmas, as well as invites readers to be midwives for the emerging religious myth that many believe to be on our collective horizon—a myth that will be more inclusive, intellectually and scientifically honest, and soul satisfying.

204 Pages
Paperback 978-1-63051-495-2 $18.95
Hardcover 978-1-63051-496-9 $29

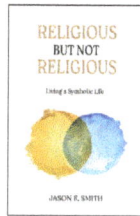

Jason E. Smith

Religious but Not Religious

Living a Symbolic Life

Jason E. Smith explores the idea, expressed by Jung, that the religious sense is a natural and vital function of the human psyche. We suffer from its lack. The symbolic forms of religion mediate unconscious and ineffable experiences to the field of consciousness that infuse our lives with meaning and purpose.

230 Pages
Paperback 978-1-63051-899-8 $21.95
Hardcover 978-1-63051-900-1 $32

Bradley A. Tepaske

Sexuality and the Religious Imagination

How could it be that the sacral significance of sex has been ignored for nearly 2,000 years of patriarchal Christian history? To address this fascinating question, TePaske surveys many classic conflicts that exist between religious creeds and the irrepressible numinosity of the body, sex and erotic love.

300 Pages
Paperback 978-1-63051-820-2 $29
Hardcover 978-1-63051-821-9 $43

SOMA & PSYCHE

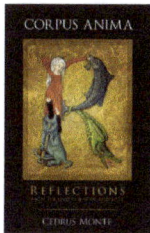

Cedrus Monte

Corpus Anima

Reflections from the Unity of Body and Soul

A collection of previously published essays written for professional Jungian journals about the unity of psyche and soma, spirit and matter, body and soul.

190 Pages
Paperback 978-1-63051-365-8 $28
Hardcover 978-1-63051-366-5 $65

TYPOLOGY

Mary E. Loomis

Dancing the Wheel of Psychological Types

A thorough, readable explanation of Jung's theory of psychological types combined with a spiritual guide adapted from Native American teachings—the medicine wheel and its beautiful inner wheels, which guide the dances of living.

128 Pages
Paperback 978-0-93302-949-1 $14.95
Hardcover
978-1-88860-295-1 $42

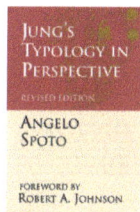

Angelo Spoto

Jung's Typology in Perspective

The Fusional Complex and the Unlived Life

In a spirited and accessible interpretation, Angelo Spoto presents at least four perspectives on Jung's philosophy of typology, including an analysis of the popular Myers-Brigg Type Indicator.

226 Pages
Paperback 978-0-93302-993-4 $27.95
Hardcover 978-1-63051-023-7 $65

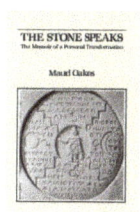

Maud Oakes

The Stone Speaks

The Memoir of a Personal Transformation

Maud Oakes's meditation on the personal and transpersonal meaning of Jung's Stone, a block of stone that he designed and carved with signs, symbols, and inscriptions that drew on Greco-Roman religious ideas and the symbolism of astrology and alchemy.

176 Pages
Available in Paperback Only
978-0-93302-904-0 $21.95

WOMEN & THE FEMININE

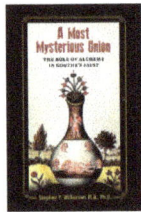

Stephen Y. Wilkerson, M.D., Ph. D.

A Most Mysterious Union

The Role of Alchemy in Goethe's Faust

This book is about hope and optimism for the future. The recorded history of our world is largely one of a sometimes worthy patriarchal striving. It has, however, all too often been tarnished, marred, and horribly disfigured by the hatreds, intolerance, and destruction that have accompanied it. And the good news? There is another way, poignantly and persuasively outlined nearly two hundred years ago by Johann Wolfgang von Goethe, involving the Divine Feminine.

384 Pages
Paperback 978-1-63051-410-5 $29
Hardcover 978-1-63051-411-2 $65

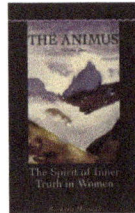

Barbara Hannah

The Animus

The Spirit of Inner Truth in Women Volume 1

This volume presents her psychological analysis of the animus, gleaned from handwritten notes, typed manuscripts, previously published articles, her own drafts of her lectures, and notes taken by those present.

328 Pages
Paperback
978-1-88860-246-3 $32
Hardcover
978-1-63051-060-2 $44.95

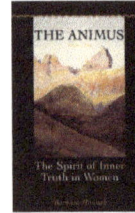

Barbara Hannah

The Animus

The Spirit of Inner Truth in Women Volume 2

Volume 2 presents her psychological analysis of the animus, gleaned from handwritten notes, typed manuscripts, previously published articles, her own drafts of her lectures, and notes taken by those present.

408 Pages
Paperback
978-1-88860-247-0 $32
Hardcover
978-1-63051-061-9 $44.95

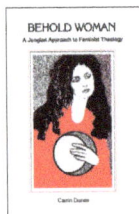

Carrin Dunne

Behold Woman

A Jungian Approach to Feminist Theology

Taking a numinous dream as her departure point, the author weaves her way through the mythological and religious amplifications of dream imagery to address issues of woman's soul and mind. She shows a feminine way of proceeding from the depth of lived experience that must undergird any approach to feminist theology.

110 Pages
Available in Paperback Only
978-0-93302-938-5 $21.95

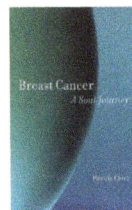

Patricia Greer

Breast Cancer

A Soul Journey

Soul Play

A Workbook to Inspire and Guide Your Soul Journey

Patricia Greer explores associations and images that surround her experience with breast cancer. A Jungian analyst, she works with metaphors and meanings related to the illness and uses her dreams, inner journeys, and poetry to deepen into and under the reality of cancer.

128 Pages
Paperback
978-1-63051-087-9 $13.95
Hardcover
978-1-63051-088-6 $47

68 Pages
Available in Paperback Only
978-1-63051-423-5 $7

Gertrudis Ostfeld de Bendayán

Ecce Mulier: Nietzsche and the Eternal Feminine

An Analytical Psychological Perspective

The author charts the developmental course of that ego, and its archetypal aspects. She has written a psychobiography that ventures into the realm of the Mothers, so that the creativity and madness of Friedrich Nietzsche can be better understood.

328 Pages
Paperback 978-1-88860-243-2 $21.95
Hardcover 978-1-63051-056-5 $42

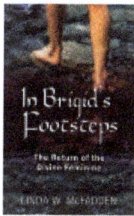

Linda McFadden

In Brigid's Footsteps
The Return of the Divine Feminine

This book focuses on the Celtic goddess and Christian saint Brigid as an archetype of the Divine Feminine. Drawing on mythology, history, and transpersonal psychology, the author traces the iconic Brigid's evolution from incarnation as goddess of wisdom, craft, and healing to embodiment as a saint of Celtic Christianity who served as midwife to Mary at the birth of Jesus.

176 Pages
Paperback 978-1-63051-956-8 $24.95
Hardcover 978-1-63051-957-5 $34

Judith Hubback

People Who Do Things to Each Other

This work shows Judith Hubback to have been able to unify her clinical and theoretic observations to a high degree of excellence. Less apparent but deeply felt, is her presence as a warm and experienced observer of all that came her way.

228 Pages
Paperback
978-0-933029-21-7 $14.95
Hardcover
978-0-933029-27-9 $42

Sylvia Shaindel Senensky

Healing and Empowering the Feminine
A Labyrinth Journey

Sylvia Senensky probes the inner depths of the labyrinth as a source of Archetypal Feminine energy: the womb, the cave, the domain of the Goddess, the core of the earth, the encounter with planned chaos, and the consequences of ignored shadow.

208 Pages
Paperback
978-1-88860-226-5 $21.95
Hardcover
978-1-63051-042-8 $42

Barbara Stevens Sullivan

Psychotherapy Grounded in the Feminine Principle

This groundbreaking book offers a proposal for approaching therapeutic work from a perspective that emphasizes the feminine principle of holding and containment, while also recognizing a necessary place for the masculine. Sullivan demonstrates the real possibility of an integrated practice with the potential to heal both men and women.

220 Pages
Paperback 978-0-93302-943-9 $28
Hardcover 978-1-88860-285-2 $65

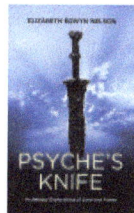

Elizabeth Eowyn Nelson

Psyche's Knife
Archetypal Explorations of Love and Power

This book examines the myth of Eros and Psyche as a metaphor for the development of soul in the psychology of women, explicating the tropes of love and power as depicted by Psyche's use of a knife in attempting to learn the identity of her lover.

192 Pages
Paperback 978-1-88860-253-1 $16.95
Hardcover 978-1-63051-066-4 $42

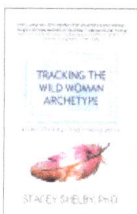

Stacey Shelby, PhD.

Tracking the Wild Woman

This book finds that the paradoxes and impossibilities of love serve to create a more profound woman who is more conscious of the manifold world of unconscious archetypes. It tracks the process of individuation and alchemical transformation through the study of texts, the author's lived experience, and imaginal ways of knowing, such as dreams, synchronicities, and active imaginations.

222 Pages
Paperback 978-1-63051-484-6 $21.95
Hardcover 978-1-63051-485-3 $42

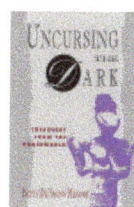

Betty De Shong Meador

Uncursing the Dark
Treasures from the Underworld

Rendered in breathtaking poetry, Betty De Shong Meador begins her exploration with the myth of Inanna's descent to the underworld. She presents this dark, psychological journey of feminine enlightenment as a positive and necessary gift of one's full individuality and creative nature.

184 Pages
Paperback 978-0-93302-965-1 $21.95
Hardcover 978-1-63051-007-7 $32

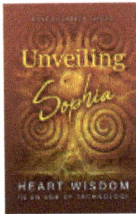

Anne Elizabeth Taylor

Unveiling Sophia

Heart Wisdom in an Age of Technology

Eternal feminine wisdom synchronizes the human heartbeat with the heartbeat of the universe. The Dalai Lama famously proclaimed that Western Women can save the world. But many modern women are painfully dissociated from Sophia, their inner spring of feminine wisdom and the primal source of their power and nurturance.

234 Pages
Paperback 978-1-63051-933-9 $27
Hardcover 978-1-63051-934-6 $37

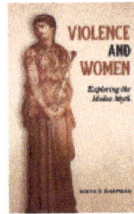

Anita S. Chapman

Violence and Women

Exploring the Medea Myth

The archetypal story of Medea is a cautionary tale for our era. Jason and Medea's marriage, favored by the gods, represents an attempt at a union of opposites very far from each other. They represent the masculine and feminine principles, covering a wide range of psychological, sociological, and historical aspects.

156 Pages
Paperback 978-1-63051-832-5 $29
Hardcover 978-1-63051-833-2 $37

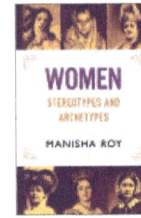

Manisha Roy

Women Stereotypes and Archetypes

The book *Women, Stereotypes and Archetypes*, by Manisha Roy, explores the complexity of modern woman's identity which is no longer supported by convenient but limiting stereotypes.

198 Pages
Paperback
978-1-63051-674-1 $21.95
Hardcover
978-1-63051-675-8 $29

Eileen H. Simon

Lady Underground's Gift

Liberating the Soul Within Us

Imagine discovering that deep within each of us exists an immensely powerful, foundational source of energy for embodying our soul's essence and for living a holistic life. Opening to this potential, influential energy for enriched development is awakening to Lady Underground, one image of the archetypal Dark Feminine, the "other side" of the Great Mother Goddess.

376 Pages
Paperback 978-1-63051-780-9 $26.95
Hardcover 978-1-63051-781-6 $42

Lena B. Ross

To Speak or Be Silent

The Paradox of Disobedience in the Lives of Women

This is an exploration of the history of the woman's dilemma in history and literature. Lena Ross has collected articles on disobedient women from Eve and Bedouin women to Jane Eyre, Dona Luz, and Virginia Woolf—how they have challenged male dominance and the structures of patriarchal oppression.

288 Pages
Paperback 978-0-93302-968-2 $27.95
Hardcover 978-1-63051-012-1 $44

Tracy Uloma Cooper

Inspired to Greatness

A Feminine Approach to Healing the World

Is it possible for a woman to be empowered and be happy? This book explores the question from a research perspective, utilizing the method of narrative analysis to examine women's one-on-one interviews. What makes this book special is the focus on the narrative voice of the women participants, which differentiates it from previous explorations and research.

100 Pages
Paperback 978-1-63051-404-4 $16.95
Hardcover 978-1-63051-405-1 $30

Lorís Simon Salum

Ensoulment

Exploring the Feminine Principle in Western Culture

Ensoulment is an encounter with young filmmaker Lorís Simón Salum as she struggles to explain the feminine, according to psychologist Carl Jung's theories.

322 Pages
Paperback 978-1-63051-389-4 $28
Hardcover 978-1-63051-390-0 $65

INDEX BY BOOK TITLE

INDEX BY AUTHOR

www.ingramcontent.com/pod-product-compliance
Lightning Source LLC
Chambersburg PA
CBHW041429270326
41933CB00026B/3495